THIS WE BELIEVE

THIS WE BELIEVE

edited by James C. Suggs

The Bethany Press
St. Louis, Missouri

Cover and Design by Roger Siebe

© **1977 by The Bethany Press**

Library of Congress Cataloguing in Publication Data
This we believe.

   1. Christian Church (Disciples of Christ)—Doctrinal and controversial works. I. Suggs, James C.
BX7321.2.T5   230'.6'63   77-23803
ISBN 0-8272-3623-9

Distributed in Canada by The G. R. Welch Company, Ltd. Toronto, Ontario, Canada
Printed in the United States of America

Foreword

What do members of the Christian Church (Disciples of Christ) believe?

That question cannot be answered finally and certainly for all of us Disciples. Beyond the fundamental affirmation that "Jesus is the Christ, the Son of the living God, and . . . (my) personal Savior," doctrinal diversity is normal in the Christian Church. Thanks to the liberty we cherish, Disciples can be found at the extremes on both the conservative right and the liberal left of Christian thought. But most of us occupy middle ground where our understandings of the Christian faith overlap considerably. In fact, many of us are eclectic, borrowing ideas from here and there. We Disciples defy neat theological classification.

This We Believe does *not* have the impossible and inappropriate task of setting down orthodoxy for Disciples. Instead, the function of this book is to stimulate additional thought with brief statements of some widely held beliefs.

Fortunately, we Disciples have shaken off our suspicion of theology (systematic thought about Christian faith). "No creed but Christ" and "No book but the Bible" are slogans expressing convictions of nineteenth-century founders of the Christian Church that are still valid. The basic point is that no human formulation of beliefs—no creed, no catechism, no official theology—should be used to separate Christians and perpetuate denominationalism. Actually, the "founding fathers"—particularly Barton W. Stone, Thomas Campbell and his son Alexander—were profound theologians. Nevertheless, for a long time the fingering of authoritative summaries of beliefs as causes of sectarianism inhibited theological thought among Disciples. We realize now that Christians can think clearly about their faith and have doctrines without being doctrinaire.

This book reflects the diversity of Disciples' thought. Few, if any, of the fifteen authors would be in complete theological agreement. Some of their differences show interestingly in what they have written. By design, *This We Believe* is a sampling—not of the extremes, but of the broad middle.

The contributors are different from one another in other-than-doctrinal ways. Among them are lay people and ordained ministers, women and men, young and "more experienced" Disciples (I'm not *about* to call any of them "old"). The ministers attended a variety of seminaries, and the lay people have diverse backgrounds. At the time they began work on their chapters, no two of the writers were living in the same region of the Christian Church. It's unlikely that any one of them knew all fourteen of the others before working on this book.

Hopefully, *This We Believe* will be useful as a springboard for individual and group study. It is sort of a companion to Kenneth L. Teegarden's 1975 book, *We Call Ourselves Disciples* (Bethany Press), which deals with what the Christian Church is like. Serious students will want to become familiar with a three-volume series of papers published in 1963 by The Bethany Press, *The Renewal of Church: The Panel of Scholars Reports*. Other substantive resources from The Bethany Press include *Journey in Faith: A History of the Christian Church (Disciples of Christ)* by Lester G. McAllister and William E. Tucker (1975) and *The Christian Church (Disciples of Christ): An Interpretative Examination in the Cultural Context* edited by George G. Beazley Jr. (1973).

None of us can say what all members of the Christian Church believe—about anything. But each of us is obligated, as one commissioned to be a witness, to understand his or her own faith well enough to say positively, "This I believe."

—James C. Suggs

Contents

God is caring, seeking, active love

Marvin Rannabargar

Your four-year-old has dropped a carton of eggs on the kitchen floor, breaking three. You've had anything but a smooth shave because your daughter used the last razor blade to cut pictures from a magazine for her science report. Your wife is in bed with the flu. In such circumstances, you hardly are wondering about the nature of God. Instead, you're concerned that somehow you get those gooey eggs cleaned up, that your wife recover fast, and that you have an extra ten minutes to stop at the drugstore for razor blades.

When, if ever, *do* we think seriously about God?

We members of the Christian Church (Disciples of Christ) definitely believe in God. Yet we do not spend many days pondering what God is like. If we were pressed for particulars about our beliefs, most of us would rely on New Testament imagery and say that God is like a father or mother to us. We feel or relate to God—in awe or ecstasy or gratitude or need or dependence. But few of us have thought out tidy doctrines of God.

My thinking about God probably is not exactly the same as yours. Indeed, I hope it isn't. Perhaps one thing we share, though, is the awareness that our understanding of the personal force at the center of life is changing—shaded and shaped by our experiences.

It is totally unlike Disciples to try to describe God and the divine-human relationship completely, absolutely and for all time. We sense that even when we have offered our best descriptions, God is greater, better, and beyond all that we have said.

We have been historically a Bible people. We have looked to the Bible for an understanding of what we believe about God, Jesus as the Christ, and other key points of faith. The biblical testimony begins with the assumption that God is: "In the beginning God . . . " (Gen. 1:1). In reading the New Testament, I have discovered that Jesus did not dialogue with philosophers, or teach formally in a classroom, or argue in any other setting about the existence of God. He assumed that existence and was terribly busy and urgent in seeking to do what he understood God wanted him to do. We Disciples characteristically start where the Bible does and where Jesus did—not with an argument, but with an affirmation.

For knowledge of what God is like, we turn first to the biblical record of God's dealings with humanity. We, the same as our spiritual forebears who produced the Old and New Testaments, hold that those historical events were self-revealing acts of God.

Old Testament Views

We recognize the Old Testament as a collection of literature covering many centuries of growing understanding of God. In Genesis we meet God the Creator, Owner and Ruler of the universe. The poetry of the Psalms rehearses and recites in moving incantation that "The heavens are telling the glory of God; and the firmament proclaims his handiwork" (Ps. 19:1). The writer of Psalm 8 reflects on the majesty of God and on the noble place humanity has been given in the creation.

In portions of the Old Testament we are told of a God who is vindictive, ruthless, jealous, almost blood-thirsty. What father today because of the evildoings of his children could drown them in a lake? Yet the whole story of Noah images a God who could, would, and did do this very thing (Gen. 6—9). In Numbers 14, Moses must intercede for his people because God wants to wipe them out for their disobedience and their desire to return to Egypt. The Book of Joshua is replete with the commands of God to destroy completely those who oppose Israel's infiltration of the "promised land."

But other Old Testament literature shows that, as the Hebrew people evolved in their spiritual thinking, their perception of God changed. Amos speaks for a God who demands that "justice roll down like waters, and righteousness like an everflowing stream" (Amos 5:24). In Micah, God is represented as one not demanding sacrifice or blood-letting, but rather requiring of man that which is good—to do justice, to love kindness and to walk humbly with God (Micah 6:8). God seems even more personal and more loving in Hosea as he refuses to forsake his wayward people: "How can I give you up, O Ephraim. . . . My heart recoils within me, my compassion grows warm and tender. I will not execute my fierce anger, I will not again destroy Ephraim; for I am God and not man, the Holy One in your midst, and I will not come to destroy" (Hosea 11:8, 9). Jeremiah is dismayed at the "word" that he must speak for the Lord, and in chapter 20 agonizes in a realization similar to that expressed by a psalmist:

> O Lord, thou hast searched me and known me!
> Thou knowest when I sit down and when I rise up;
> > thou discernest my thoughts from afar.
>
> • • •
>
> Even before a word is on my tongue,
> > lo, O lord, thou knowest it altogether.
>
> • • •
>
> Whither shall I go from my Spirit?
> > Or whither shall I flee from thy presence?
>
> • • •
>
> Search me, O God, and know my heart!
> Try me and know my thoughts!
>
> • • •
>
> and lead me in the way everlasting!
> —Ps. 139:1-2, 4, 7, 23, 24.

It is in the New Testament representation of Jesus, however, that Christians find the unique revelation of God. Jesus himself said, "He who has seen me has seen the Father" (John 14:9).

The Bible, then, is the story not of humanity's search for God, but of God's reaching out to people. The Old Testament tells of a God who created everything; who led and made a covenant with Israel; who despised unfaithfulness but showed compassion; who used patriarchs, judges, kings, and prophets for his purposes; who would not give up and let go. The New Testament reports that "the Word became flesh and dwelt among us" (John 1:14), and presents Jesus as evidence of the length to which God will go to restore a relationship with the creation. Paul wrote it this way: "God was in Christ reconciling the world to himself" (2 Cor. 5:19). Believing that God has come to us in Jesus, we look to his teachings and activities for knowledge against which all other concepts of God, including those from the Old Testament, must be tested.

"Father" Who Cares

Speaking in intimate terms about his own relationship with "my Father," Jesus communicated the wonder that God cares for each of us. He said that even the hairs on our heads are counted. (Admittedly, for some that would be an easy task, but for the rest—that takes a lot of counting!) He told us that not even a sparrow drops, not even the smallest of the birds dies without God knowing of it! He taught us to pray, "Our Father . . . ," trusting God to be aware of and responsive to our needs.

Jesus told three stories to illustrate how much God cares for individuals "lost" in various ways.[1] One concerned a woman who, having lost a coin, swept and moved furniture until she found that coin. (God hunts for us in the same way.) Another story was about a shepherd who left a flock of ninety-nine sheep to find one lost in the wilds and bring it back. (God cares enough for us personally first to know when we are lost, then to go out looking for us and carry us gently into the safety of the fold.)

In the third parable, which was even more exhaustive, Jesus told of a boy who became sick and tired of living in the shelter of his father and in the shadow of his older brother. "Give me what I'll get after you die," the boy said to his father, "that I may go into the world and seek fame and fortune." His father willingly let him leave with his inheritance. Before long, the boy fell into bad company. His friends lasted as long as his money. He ended up on a pig farm slopping the hogs in order to get a little to eat. He came to himself. He started home. His father, who in the eyes of the community had been shamed by his son's actions, went to meet his returning son, thus protecting him from the others' wrath. He hugged the young man, lifted him up, killed a fatted calf and held a big barbecue as a homecoming present. "My son, who was lost, is found!" he exclaimed. (God cares for us even when we are off squandering our inheritance; even when we are wasting our talents, our time, our futures—still God cares. And if and when we come to ourselves, God will receive us back with celebrating.)

Such teachings, coupled with the self-giving ministry of Jesus, reveal a seeking God who actively moves toward us. God came to us in Jesus to show us his love, to show us that he cares,[2] to show us that he wants to heal our sick lives, to show us that he would bind up our broken hearts, to show us that he even would give us the freedom to run away, always to be received back. We believe that God cares for us.

But God is not content to let us rummage through the Bible discovering how and what he is. He comes to us very often in the lives and through the lives of others. God moves mysteriously in many lives.

One such person was Bess Cunningham, a spirit who cared. She was a retired nurse when I knew her as a seminary pastor to the Christian Church at Granger, Iowa. I remember her writing to the church's general offices wondering if there might be a place for her to train nurses or a mission station where she could nurse. She was too old. But that did not stop Bess. She sorted stamps. She sorted through the lives of so many in that small Iowa community—not as a busybody but as one serving in the spirit of Christ. Fresh bread, a concerned inquiry, an

---

1. The paraphrases and interpretations that follow are based on a trilogy of parables contained in the fifteenth chapter of Luke.

2. It is virtually impossible to write or speak of God without using personal pronouns, which have gender. They have been avoided, however, until this paragraph. Use of the masculine gender does not mean that all Disciples should or do think of God as male. The alternative in this paragraph would have been to alternate, using two "he's" and two "she's," which possibly would have hindered rather than helped communication.

offer to take someone shopping, even a little extra money—such were the forms of her caring. She always went beyond the second mile. God was with Bess. Her life spoke of God's giving, sharing, continual caring. God touched my life and hundreds of other lives through Bess Cunningham.

You and I can think of countless persons who have exemplified the spirit of Christ and been the instruments of God within the world. God continues to come and reveal himself through the great and the small today. In this I find my capacity for belief strengthened.

Active in the World

While we think of God as spirit, still we do not believe that God has nothing to do with the world of which we are a part. To the contrary, we fully expect to encounter God in the midst of the stuff and the events of the world. In that sense, we believe in a very material God. God is in the actions of nations. God is in the movements of persons seeking freedom. God is in governmental workings and decisions. God is found through the daily newspaper, as well as through the sacred collection of writings we label "Holy Bible." God is in the affairs of his creation leading people toward justice, righteousness, reconciliation.

We have the tendency to try to box God into the church so that his Spirit can only peek out through our stained-glass windows and walnut arches. But God continually breaks out of our "god boxes." He is always beyond our definitions. He is always beyond even our expectations, stalking the quiet, shadowed places of this planet where hunger burns, where need is pregnant, where suffering persists.

God always moves before us. He moves ahead of the church, ahead even of the greatest social schemes or evilest of armament races. We know that God is shaping the destiny of our world. We believe that he is involved in the confrontations that continually rage between good and evil. And we are certain that God will prevail. A part of our pilgrimage in faith is to discover through eyes that see, through ears that hear, and through hearts that understand what God is up to within the world.

From our clear view of God in Jesus caring and seeking, from our glimpses of the same spirit in persons around us, and from our observation of God's constant involvement with the world, we would conclude that God is love in action: that is basic to our understanding of God. The Gospels and the letters of John in the New Testament are replete with this characterization of God. The heart of our good news is found in John 3:16: "For God so loved the world that he gave his only Son, that whoever believes in him should not perish but have eternal life." In the fourth chapter of First John this concept is expanded:

> Beloved, let us love one another; for love is of God, and he who loves is born of God and knows God. . . . Beloved, if God so loved us, we also ought to love one another. . . . So we know and believe the love God has for us. God is love, and he who abides in love abides in God, and God abides in him. . . . We love, because he first loved us (vs. 7, 11, 16, 19).

God is love! God is love in action. God is that activity within the world, the ground of all being, the source of all life, that exists as energetic and powerful love. God is spirit. And when we are imbued with that strength, that power, that spirit, which is love, and express it in all that we have and are and want to be, then we are even more truly the children of God.

Love is an overworked word in today's vocabulary, but it is never an overworked activity within the world. We believe that God is that motivating love that sparks our outward movement toward and with others, and keeps sane that inward movement of life in the quiet places.

Marvin Rannabargar serves in the heart of the campus of Illinois State University as minister of University Christian Church of Normal.

His previous pastorates were in Brookfield, Wisconsin; Du Quoin, Illinois; and Hannibal, Missouri, where he was an associate. He also served for one year as acting librarian of the Drake University Divinity School.

Secretary of the executive board of the United Campus Christian Foundation in Normal, Mr. Rannabargar is a former board chairman of United Ministries in Higher Education at the University of Wisconsin in Milwaukee.

In the Christian Church in Illinois and Wisconsin, he is a member of the leader development commission and chairman of the 1978 regional assembly task force. He also is co-dean of a cluster chapter of the regional College of Ministers.

A native of Missouri, Mr. Rannabargar earned a B.A. degree from Culver-Stockton College and a M.Div. degree from the Drake Divinity School. He has contributed articles to *The Disciple, The Bethany Guide* and *Culver-Stockton Concept.*

Jesus Christ is Lord and Savior

James K. Hempstead

"No creed but Christ" has been the basic position of the Christian Church from its inception. As a consequence, no official statement has ever been adopted or imposed as a basis for membership.

On the other hand, every person who seeks membership in the church is asked some variation of the simple question, "Do you believe that Jesus is the Christ, the Son of the living God, and do you accept him as Savior and Lord?"

This precise wording does not appear in the Scriptures. It has its primary source in Peter's declaration at Caesarea Philippi, "You are the Christ, the Son of the living God" (Matt. 16:16). It also is suggested by a passing observation of Paul when he wrote to the Corinthians that "no one can say 'Jesus is Lord' except by the Holy Spirit" (1 Cor. 12:3), and in the marginal reading included in the story of the conversion of the Ethiopian who confessed, "I believe that Jesus Christ is the Son of God" (Acts 8:37).

What do we Disciples of Christ believe about Jesus? It is set forth in the familiar words of the so-called Good Confession, i.e., "We believe that Jesus is the Christ, the Son of the living God, and we accept him as Savior and Lord."

It is understandable that the interest of biblical scholars and archaeologists was whetted keen when areas known to have been frequented by early Christians repeatedly revealed the outlines of fish—scrawled in lamp-black on the rocky corridors of the catacombs or scratched with some sharp tool on the wall of a humble dwelling. What could this mean?

Unexpectedly the hidden truth leaped to the surface: the sign of the fish was a symbolic testimony of Christian faith. The five letters that spell the Greek word for fish are the first letters of the key five words in the Good Confession. The Greek word is *IXΘUS*—*iota, chi, theta, upsilon* and *sigma*. The five words in the confession of faith are *'Iesoûs, Christós, theoû, huiós, sotér,* or "I believe that *Jesus* is the *Christ,* the *Son* of *God,* my *Savior.*" Wherever the sign of the fish was drawn—even in the dust by some faithful, but cautious Christian— someone was declaring to the world, "This is where I stand. This I believe!"

Real Person of Record

If nothing else, the sign of the fish and the words it symbolizes declare to all who see or hear a *faith in the fact of Jesus.* The first letter is *iota;* the first word is *'Iesoûs* (Jesus).

The personality of Jesus, as portrayed in the Gospels, is so vivid, and his individual characteristics are so distinct that we get the impression of a real man making an intense impact upon real people in an actual historical situation. This fact notwithstanding, some have thought that Jesus of Nazareth never existed—that he was only a myth—and that Christianity, like some other religions, was built on legend. Thoughtful men have therefore asked, "To which category does the Christian faith belong?" The sign of the fish declares that Jesus belongs to the realm of fact.

Had Jesus never really lived, none would have known it better than the Jews. Had it been possible, they surely would have raised the issue. On the contrary, however, all of their attacks upon Jesus took for granted that he lived, taught, and died in Palestine.

The Jewish Talmud contains an early reference to Jesus. While scholars consider certain phrases to be later interpolations, they concur in the fact that reference is there made to a real, flesh-and-blood individual:

> On the eve of the Passover, Jesus of Nazareth was hanged. During forty days a herald went before him crying aloud, "He ought to be stoned because he has practiced magic, has led Israel astray, and caused them to rise in rebellion. Let him who has something to say in his defense come forward and declare it." But no one came forward, and he was hanged on the eve of the Passover.[1]

Other Jewish writings are equally clear. Of all the charges his enemies hurled at Jesus, one thing no one ever did was suggest that he never existed.

---

1. This quotation from the Talmud and the following references are discussed at length in *Jesus of Nazareth* by Joseph Klausner, translated by Herbert Danby. Copyright 1925 by Macmillan Publishing Co., Inc., renewed 1953 by Herbert Danby, pp. 27ff. Used by permission.

The same is true concerning evidence in the writings of certain early Romans. The references are few. But there were many new religions abroad then, and one hardly would expect extended discourses on what appeared to be only a passing reform movement in Judaism.

This fact notwithstanding, Tacitus, writing about A.D. 115, describes Nero's ruse when, in A.D. 64, he blamed the burning of Rome on the "Christians." Tacitus adds, "This name comes from Christ, whom the procurator Pontius Pilate, under the rule of Tiberius, had handed over to torture."

About the same time, Pliny the Younger wrote about meetings where hymns were sung to "one Christus as a god"; while Suetonius wrote a full fifty years earlier how the Emporer Claudius banished from Rome the Jews "who made a great tumult because of Crestus."

Whenever Jewish or Roman writers refer to Jesus, they take for granted his historic existence; confirm some detail of his life, ministry or death; and breathe not the faintest rumor that he was a legendary figure.

The Christian faith is founded upon fact—the fact of Jesus of Nazareth about whom we read in the New Testament and elsewhere—the fact of Jesus of Nazareth whose historicity never is questioned, even by his enemies. The Jesus whom we find on the pages of the New Testament is no passing phantom; he is a real person. The sign of the fish, like the Christian faith, is founded upon the fact of Jesus.

Instrument for Redemption

The second letter in the Greek word for fish is *chi*. The second word in the Good Confession is *Christôs* i.e., "Christ." This Jesus who was crucified is *the Christ, the deliverer of mankind.*

It is altogether possible that many do not clearly understand what the word "Christ" denotes. Habit has allowed us to use the word interchangeably with "Jesus." Actually it is a title or designation, falling in the same category with such expressions as "Jesus, the Nazarene," "Jesus, the son of Mary" or "Jesus, the carpenter."

The word "Christ" means "the Anointed," "the Chosen One" or "the Divine Instrument." When we affirm our belief in Jesus as the Christ, we are declaring that he is God's chosen instrument for the redemption of the world.

The sign of the fish proclaims that Jesus embodies God's supreme effort to break through the barriers of man's indifference and sin. He is the Christ, the Messiah, the Chosen One of God.

It is not difficult to see why the Jewish people were disappointed in him. Laboring under the yoke of Roman bondage and steeped in certain Old Testament scriptures which promised a great deliverer, they sought someone who would be another King David. They longed for a leader who would set up a theocratic monarchy and exercise political force. This meant revolution and war, possibly freedom.

When Jesus appeared, saying that his kingdom was "not of this world," they casually ignored him. When he prophesied that the temple, the symbol of Jewish solidarity and continuity, would be destroyed, they could not endure him. It was soon easier to do away with him than to wrestle with his new ideas.

The Jews wanted an earthly ruler who would establish an earthly kingdom, but Jesus did not fit this mold. He was the promised Deliverer, but in an altogether different sense.

We therefore believe, as our Good Confession states, that Jesus is the Christ, God's Chosen Instrument for mankind's redemption, but in a far broader sense than that of a narrow nationalistic ruler. Basic to our faith and implicit in the sign of the fish is the fact that Jesus is humanity's highest hope, the Chosen One of God.

Revelation of God

The third and fourth letters in the Greek word for fish are *theta* and *upsilon*, while the third and fourth key words in the so-called Good Confession are *theoû* and *huiós:* "of God the Son!" We believe that Jesus is the Christ, *the Son of God.*

> The nameless writer to the Hebrews begins thus:
> In many and various ways God spoke of old to our fathers by the prophets; but in these last days he has spoken to us by a Son. . . . He reflects the glory of God and bears the very stamp of his nature (1:1-2, 3).

In other words, Jesus is God's Son, revealing God's likeness, his attributes, his concerns.

To be sure, Jesus cannot present the whole of God within the limitations of human existence, but he can present in human form a character that may be understood, admired, loved, respected, feared, even hated. Those who accept this claim find that Jesus is the small opening through which we can glimpse something of the immensity and magnificence of the Eternal. Nothing in all the world either outstrips or outmodes the God who is revealed in Jesus Christ, his Son.

It would be a mistake to suppose that God is no "bigger" or "greater" (if such words be permitted) than Jesus of Nazareth, limited as he was by time, space, and circumstance. But the greatest ideas of God we can conceive arrange themselves without question or incongruity around those traits revealed by Jesus.

"No one has ever seen God," John writes in the opening section of the Gospel that bears his name; "the only Son, who is in the bosom of the Father, he has made him known" (1:18). Nothing is more basic to the truth of the Christian gospel. If Jesus' claim to divine sonship is disallowed, we are dealing with a religious racketeer. We can neither trust his teachings nor depend upon his integrity.

Fortunately, both the experience of those who encountered him long ago and the testimony of those who know him now affirm that he *does* enjoy a special relationship with God—that he reveals and speaks for him in an utterly distinctive way—that he is a phenomenon without precedent on the world scene.

If as "the Son of God," Jesus gives us a glimpse of what God himself is like, he also draws us a living picture of what other "sons of God" such as ourselves can become. And if our first reaction on beholding him is "I am not like that," then our second is surely "This is what I *ought* to be and *can* be." We Disciples treasure the truth set forth in John's observation that "to all who received him, who believed in his name, he gave power to become children of God" (John 1:12).

John Hunter's familiar lines express the dream which can now become reality because of Jesus' life and ministry:

> Dear Master, in whose life I see
>   All that I would, but fail to be;
> Let thy clear light forever shine,
>   To shame and guide this life of mine.
>
> Though what I dream and what I do
>   In my weak days are always two,
> Help me, oppressed by things undone,
>   O Thou, whose deeds and dreams were one![2]

The words "Son of God" imply a uniqueness of relationship and mission. Jesus came not only to make God known, but also to make men and women aware of the design after which they can successfully pattern their lives. We respond favorably to this. We therefore declare our faith in Jesus as the Christ, the Son of God.

Savior and Lord

And we accept him as our Savior. The fifth letter in the word for fish is *sigma* which is the initial letter in the Greek word *sotér,* meaning "Savior."

Everyone needs a Savior. We need to be saved *from* our sins, from our failures, from our low aims and from ourselves. We need to be saved *to* a new birth, a fresh beginning through which we can lay legitimate claims to our spiritual birthrights.

As has always been true, there is current today a philosophy which asserts that men and women, by their own strength and ingenuity, will finally overcome the problems of the world. It holds that God is expendable in the struggle with those issues that face humanity.

While the usual expression of this point of view may not put it quite this bluntly, it does declare that those who lean upon God are weak, insipid, less than what they ought to be. Who needs a Savior—something or "Someone Other"—to direct and have lordship over his life?

A person needs but read the blurbs on the jackets of the flood of books rolling from publishers' presses to illustrate this. Written by all kinds of people—some with considerable skill, others almost devoid of insight—each of these volumes purports to look realistically at the quagmire in which we have become en-

---

2. John Hunter, "Dear Master, in Whose Life I See."

trapped. They are filled with all sorts of formulae and blueprints, with "do-it-yourself" schemes by the score. Their recurring theme is that one can lift oneself by the bootstraps from the moral morass that drags downward. Each author's thesis seems to be that if each of us would just give one final "heave-ho, my hearties!" salvation would be just around the corner.

Unfortunately the history of civilization reveals that is untrue. Mankind cannot exist, much less triumph, without reference to God.

In times of personal and national tragedy, anyone is bereft of hope with no resources other than himself or herself. No humanistic "heave-ho, my hearties!" can fulfill the deepest needs of the human soul. Only God in Christ can bring salvation which, essentially, is wholeness, soundness, and health. That salvation becomes real and fills life with power when any penitent believer accepts Jesus as both Savior and Lord.

> Make me a captive, Lord,
> And then I shall be free;
> Force me to render up my sword,
> And I shall conqueror be.
>
> I sink in life's alarms
> When by myself I stand;
> Imprison me within thine arms,
> And strong shall be my hand.[3]

This, then, is what we believe about Jesus of Nazareth. It is suggested by the acrostic composed of the Greek letters for the word "fish." We believe that Jesus was a real person who lived and walked among men. We affirm that he is the Christ, the long-awaited Deliverer of mankind. We insist that, as God's Son, he sustains a special relationship with God—that in the deepest sense "God was in Christ reconciling the world to himself" (2 Cor. 5:19). But best of all, we Disciples are assured that he can be our personal Savior and Lord.

> If you confess with your lips that Jesus is Lord and believe in your heart that God raised him from the dead, you will be saved. For man believes with his heart and so is justified, and he confesses with his lips and so is saved (Rom. 10:9-10).

"No creed but Christ"—but what a creed! What a Lord and Savior!

---

3. George Matheson (1842-1906), "Make Me a Captive, Lord."

James K. Hempstead is senior minister of East Dallas (Texas) Christian Church.

First vice-moderator of the Christian Church during the 1975-77 biennium, Dr. Hempstead has had numerous church responsibilities at regional and general levels. He has been a member of the Disciples' General Board and its Administrative Committee since 1969. Another major involvement has been his service since 1965 on the board of directors of the Christian Board of Publication.

Dr. Hempstead's previous pastorates were with First Christian Church, Ames, Iowa; First Christian Church, Centralia, Illinois; First Christian Church, Alhambra, California; and Central Woodward Christian Church, Detroit, Michigan.

Noted as a preacher, he has keen interest in evangelism. His sermons have appeared in *Pulpit Magazine* and he has contributed articles to various religious publications.

Reared in Oklahoma, he earned a B.A. degree from Phillips University and a B.D. degree from the Graduate Seminary there. He has done further study at four seminaries and holds honorary degrees from Phillips and Bethany College.

God works through the Holy Spirit

David R. Darnell

In the fall of 1974, a group of Christian Church leaders met in a North Carolina regional study conference on evangelism. Included were two of our regional ministers, a professor of religion from Atlantic Christian College, and a representative group of ordained ministers and lay leaders. Out of that conference came a statement which included the following affirmation of faith:

We believe in the Holy Spirit. God, the Creator, Who has come to us, and revealed Himself to us in Jesus Christ, is still present with us today through the Holy Spirit. It is the Holy Spirit within us that causes us to cry out for God, and that convicts us of our sin. As we commit our lives to Jesus Christ in Christian baptism, the Holy Spirit is given to us, filling our lives with power, giving us new life and direction, and imparting rich gifts for service and mission. Especially, as we read and study the Bible, the Holy Spirit speaks to us through its words, recreating us into the People of God, strengthened and guided by God, and set apart for God's purpose and mission.

As one of the drafters of that statement, I was and am convinced that it is true—biblically and experientially, and from a philosophical theological standpoint as well.

To show the validity of this statement, I will deal with just two of many biblical texts that could be considered, using my own translations in order to arrest attention and break open the meaning of the texts.[1]

The first text, Isaiah 63:7-14, comes from a collection of prophecies which affirm the exalted transcendence of God (see Isa. 57:15, 63:15 and 66:1-2); yet this passage declares that God has been and is actively present in human history through his "Holy Spirit":

I will call to memory the lovingkindnesses of Yahweh,
    the praises of Yahweh;
according to all (the ways in) which Yahweh has dealt with us,
    and (His) great goodness to the House of Israel.
Because He has dealt with them according to His (motherly)
      compassion,
    and according to the multitude of His loving kindnesses!

And He said, "Surely they are My people—
children (who) will not be deceptive!"
And He was to them a Savior:
    in all their distress, not a distress but[2] the Angel
      of His Presence saved them;
    in His love and in His mercy He redeemed them;
    and He lifted them up, and carried them, all the days of old.

But they rebelled,
    and grieved His Holy Spirit.[3]
And He was changed toward them, (becoming) an Enemy;
    He Himself fought against them.

And (then) He remembered the days of old—
    Moses, (and) His people.
Where is the One Who brings them up from the sea,

---

1. The author, a student of the Hebrew Bible and the Greek New Testament for more than twenty-five years, teaches and preaches directly from the Hebrew and Greek texts. Since it is his style, personal pronouns representing Deity are capitalized. In the translations on this page and of John 14—16, words not actually found in the original text are placed in parentheses. For reviews of the biblical usage of "Spirit" (*Ruah, Pneuma*), see G. W. H. Lampe's article "Holy Spirit" in *The Interpreter's Dictionary of the Bible*, Vol. II, pp. 626-30 (Abingdon Press), and the very technical article by H. Kleinknecht, F. Baumgaertel, W. Bieder, E. Sjoeberg and E. Schweitzer, "Pneuma . . . ," in *Theological Dictionary of the New Testament*, Vol. VI. Eerdmans, 1969, pp. 332-451.
2. Or "He was distressed and" instead of "not a distress but."
3. Compare Ephesians 4:30.

with the shepherds of His flock?
Where is the One Who places in His (people's) midst
His Holy Spirit?[4]
(Where is He) Who leads at the right hand of Moses,
(with) His glorious arm?
(Where is He) Who divides waters from before them,
to make for Himself an everlasting name?
(Where is He) Who leads them through the (fearful) deeps,
like a horse through the desert?
They will not stumble;
like cattle going down (safely) through the valley,
Yahweh's Spirit[5] will give us rest!

Here, Israel confesses God's deeds of saving love while confessing her own guilt. God has been deeply involved with Israel throughout her history either as Savior or as Enemy, depending on Israel's choices freely made. When Israel rebelled, she was rebelling against and causing pain to God's Holy Spirit (or "spirit of His holiness"), which God "places in their midst." In the whole experience of deliverance from bondage and entrance into "rest" (their new home of peace and prosperity in the Promised Land), it is Yahweh's Spirit that leads them into and gives them "rest."[6]

Thus, God is not seen in the Old Testament as standing in splendid isolation from his people. Rather, the transcendent God is viewed as dynamically present in and through his Holy Spirit—both in the ancient past and in the living present, and in the hoped-for future as well.

In correspondence with this, the varied writings of the Old Testament view the Spirit as the universal source of life, both human and animal,[7] and as the active instrument of God in his people's history. As the Old Testament looks into the future, it sees the hoped-for new age as preeminently an "age of the Spirit" in which the messianic King will be the bearer of God's Spirit[8] and in which the people of God will be given a new heart through the presence of the Spirit in their midst.[9]

Empowering Presence

The New Testament claims that the messianic King, who is the bearer and imparter of the Holy Spirit, has entered into human history in Jesus of Nazareth (see Mark 1:8, 10; Luke 4:16-21) and that in his ministry, the Holy Spirit is at

---

4. Compare Nehemiah 9:20.
5. Compare Psalms 143:10
6. The tense of the verbs in Hebrew is significant. The ancient story is "updated"; what happened in the past is being relived and experienced in the present.
7. See W. Eichrodt, *Theology of the Old Testament*. The Westminster Press, 1967, Vol. II, p. 48. Used by permission.
8. See Isaiah 11:2.
9. See especially Ezekiel 11:19-20, 36:26-27.

work bringing near the kingdom of God (Mark 3:28-30, Luke 11:20). The disciples of Jesus are incapable, on their own, of following him on his way to the cross (Mark 14:27-31); it is only after he has given himself as a "ransom for many" (Mark 10:45), and later has met them as their risen Lord, that they will be able to follow him in his way of self-giving ministry (Mark 16:1-8). For, as the risen, exalted Lord, he will be with them (Matt. 28:18-20). This presence of the risen Lord with his disciples is pictured in Luke-Acts as fulfilled in the coming of the Holy Spirit on the disciples (Acts 1—2). In Paul, this amazing new source of life and power is summed up in the phrase "in Christ" (see 2 Cor. 5:17). The earthly, physically limited Jesus is gone; but the risen Lord is present in his Holy Spirit, convicting and convincing the world, teaching and guiding the disciples, imparting manifold gifts for ministry and giving birth to the wonderful "fruit of the Spirit" (Gal. 5:16-26), the greatest of which is love (1 Cor. 13; see chaps. 12—14). In John 14—16, this promise of the Holy Spirit's presence is made especially clear:

> And I will ask the Father, and He will give you another *Paraclete* ("Helper," "Intercessor"), in order that It[10] may be with you forever, the Spirit of truth, which the world is not able to receive, because it does not see It, nor know (It). You know It, because It remains with you and is in you. I will not leave you orphans; I am coming to you. (14:16-18.)
> . . . When the *Paraclete* shall come, which I will send to you from the Father, the Spirit of truth, which comes out from the Father, that One will testify concerning Me. (15:26.)
> . . . But I tell you the truth, it is profitable for you that I am going away. For if I do not go away, the *Paraclete* will not come to you. But if I do go away, I will send It to you. And when that One has come, It will convict (or "expose the guilt of") the world concerning sin and concerning righteousness and concerning judgment. Concerning sin, that is, because they do not believe in Me; and concerning righteousness, because I am going away to the Father, and you no longer see Me; and concerning judgment, because the ruler of this world has been condemned.
> I still have many things to say to you, but you are not able to bear (them) at this time. But when that One has come, the Spirit of truth, It will guide you in(to) the whole truth. (16:7-13.)

John's Gospel teaches that the risen, exalted Lord will be physically absent from his disciples, yet will be mysteriously present with them in the *Paraclete* ("Helper," "Intercessor"), which John identifies as the "Spirit of truth" or "Holy Spirit." The Spirit's presence is synonymous with Jesus' own presence, and also with the Father's presence. It will be with Jesus' disciples forever, distinguishing their life from the "world's" life and convicting or exposing the guilt of the world with regard to sin, righteousness, and judgment.

---

10. "The Spirit" in Greek is neither masculine nor feminine, but neuter in gender. Thus, the pronouns used to refer to the Spirit throughout John 14-16 are neuter in gender and should be so translated.

Threefold Work

This threefold work of the Holy Spirit has caused much difficulty to interpreters of John 14—16.[11] As described in this passage, the ongoing work of the Spirit is linked closely with the historical work of Jesus. Its revelation is not a "new" revelation, but rather is a constant bringing to memory and application of the revelation of God already given in Jesus. The world will be brought into confrontation with the meaning of Jesus' life, teaching, death, and life beyond death through the work of the Holy Spirit in Jesus' disciples.

It will convict the world concerning sin: Jesus, as the embodiment of love for God and neighbor, will be the basis by which the Holy Spirit in the disciples will convict the unbelieving world of its "missing of the mark," of its sin. The world's faithless life, in contrast with the example of the great Lord of Life, will come to know how "off center" it is.

It will convict the world concerning righteousness: The fact that death was not the final end for Jesus, but that rather he is risen and exalted (has gone away to the Father), will convict the world of the righteousness of his cause. It will show that his way of self-giving ministry even unto death is in reality God's true righteousness, the only way to life and hope for the entire world.

It will convict the world concerning judgment: The Holy Spirit in the disciples will confront the world with the Word embodied in Jesus, thereby calling the world into judgment/decision by that Word, and making known the truth which is the only real basis for human judgment. In the events surrounding the historical Jesus, the evil world powers have been shown once and for all in their weakness and folly. The Holy Spirit will take these things of Jesus and guide the disciples into their interpretation and application, thereby reaching out to the whole unbelieving world with the revelation of God the Father in Jesus the Christ.

Certainly there is strong evidence from the Bible of the promise that the Holy Spirit will be present with the disciples—giving new life, strengthening, teaching, guiding, imparting gifts for mission. But is this promise true in our own experience as Disciples of Christ?[12]

If a poll were taken of Disciples today, an outsider probably would be amazed at the diversity of answers which would be given to this question. On the one hand, there would be the young deacon in one of our Texas congregations who stated that he had never even heard about the Holy Spirit and who expressed resentment that such an omission had been made in his religious training. On the other hand there would be the wife of a Disciples minister in North Carolina who has been "baptized in the Holy Spirit" and who rejoices in her newfound gift of "speaking in tongues." Somewhere between these two would be found the majority of Disciples: having been taught in varying degrees concerning the

---

11. See Raymond Brown, *The Gospel According to John (XIII-XXI)* (Doubleday & Company, Inc., 1970) for a very helpful overall treatment of these three chapters.

12. See Stephen J. England's "The Holy Spirit in the Thought and Life of the Disciples of Christ," *The Reformation of Tradition*, ed. Ronald E. Osborn, Vol. I, *The Renewal of Church: The Panel of Scholars Reports*. The Bethany Press, 1963, pp. 112-134.

Holy Spirit, and interpreting their own religious pilgrimages in diverse ways as evidence of the presence of the Spirit in human experience.

And while it is true that some of us have had little or no experience that we can interpret as validating the biblical promise of the presence of the Holy Spirit, it also is true that this is by no means the unanimous or even the majority experience of Disciples today, and certainly not in Disciples history. Rather, in the birth of the Disciples movement on the frontier, the experience of the reality of the Holy Spirit's presence was common to "Christian" and "Disciples" roots. And throughout our history, the large majority of Disciples have confessed the reality of the Holy Spirit's presence in convicting power, especially through the preaching of the Good News, in the renewing cleansing associated with baptism, and in high moments of Christian worship, devotion, and mission.

Differences in Experience

But however we may answer this question of our Disciples heritage in a general way, the matter of experience demands from each of us a personal response. I have sensed the Spirit's presence in powerful, challenging ways throughout my Christian pilgrimage. In my baptism, renewal, forgiveness and strength came into my life. In my ordination, a new sense of the presence of the Holy Spirit entered into my ministry. Time and again, although there have been long "dry" spells, the refreshing renewal and cleansing of the Holy Spirit has been felt, giving power, guidance and understanding, and opening doors of opportunity for ministry.

Our greatest danger, I believe, with reference to the Holy Spirit is the constant danger of pulling apart into opposing camps on the basis of our differences in experience. In order to avert this danger, those of us who have had little experience which we can claim as evidence of the Holy Spirit in our lives should open ourselves to the reality of this biblical promise. Are there no gifts which we may well have overlooked as evidences of God's presence? What about life itself, the air we breathe? What about our love for God and for our neighbors; what about our abilities to serve? Similarly, those of us who have had deep, thrilling experiences of the Holy Spirit's reality should guard against the always-present danger of religious pride. We should resist thinking that unless people have shared in our identical experience, they have been overlooked by the Spirit!

So we can say that this belief in the Holy Spirit is based solidly in biblical theology and in human religious experience. What can we say about it from the standpoint of philosophical theology? Here, the words "transcendence" and "immanence" play a major role. Philosophical theology has moved from one extreme to the other—sometimes stressing the radical transcendence of God, sometimes favoring the total immanence of God. Views of God still range between the extremes of "deism" and "pantheism." Some say "no miracles"; others "everything is miracle."

The beauty of seeing God as working in human history through the Holy Spirit is that such a view combines transcendence with immanence. It preserves the majesty, the exaltation of Almighty God while confessing him as active in every time and place, especially in those specific revelatory events in the history of Israel surrounding Moses, the prophets and Jesus of Nazareth. God is seen in his paradoxical reality: exalted far above the universe in matchless splendor and at the same time close to his lowly creation, to every hair of our heads and every sparrow that falls; present even at the subatomic level of reality.

And so I, as one Disciple of Christ, can join with my fellow Disciples in affirming:

> We believe in the Holy Spirit. God, the Creator, Who has come to us, and revealed Himself to us in Jesus Christ, is still present with us today through the Holy Spirit. . . .

David R. Darnell is pastor of First Christian Church in Perryton, Texas. Before assuming that pastorate in mid-1977, he had been minister of First Christian Church in Fayetteville, North Carolina, for 15 years.

Involved in diverse aspects of ministry, Dr. Darnell has been Bible lecturer at many regional and national gatherings of the Christian Church (Disciples of Christ). He was co-founder of the Fayetteville Family Life Center, the Fayetteville Contact Teleministry and the Cumberland County Day Activity Center—all ecumenical. He also has been director of summer camping programs for the under-privileged and the retarded.

In 1973, he received a Ph.D. degree in biblical studies from Duke University. He previously had earned a B.A. degree from Florida Christian College and a B.D. degree from Texas Christian University's Brite Divinity School, and studied Greek and Hebrew at the University of Toronto.

The church is people embodying Christ

William C. Howland Jr.

Most of us remember or played the finger game that goes:

> Here is the church;
> Here is the steeple.
> Open the doors—
> See all the people!

This childhood lore calls our attention to a fact often obscured: *The church is people*. Ask almost anyone to show you the church. You probably will be directed to a building at a particular location—say, 21st at University—labeled "Christian," or "Presbyterian," or "Methodist." But the church is not a building; it is people! It is not on a corner in any given place; it is everywhere people are.

This understanding of the church as people is conveyed by the New Testament itself. The letters of Paul and other writers are not addressed to buildings, but begin, "To all . . . God's people . . . who live at Philippi" or "To God's people in Ephesus" (NEB). Christian scriptures contain no descriptions of first-century meeting places, but rather reports of the experiences and insights of people who composed the church. We members of the Christian Church say proudly that we take our concept of the church from the New Testament. Thus, we begin with the affirmation that *the church is people.*

Still, the church is more than just any kind of people: *the church is a peculiar people.* Not peculiar in the sense of strange or odd, although they may sometimes appear so, but peculiar in what distinguishes church people from others. The church is composed of persons who are committed to faith in God through the lordship of Jesus Christ. This commitment sets those who acknowledge Christ as Son of God and Savior apart from those who ignore or deny him, or accept him in other categories, i.e., ethicist, teacher, prophet, fanatic or fraud. They are "Christ-ian"—belonging to Christ. So the New Testament letters are addressed "To God's people . . . who are faithful in their life in union with Christ Jesus" (Eph. 1:1 TEV) or "to all who are called to be God's holy people, who belong to him in union with Christ Jesus, together with all people everywhere who worship our Lord Jesus Christ, their Lord and ours" (1 Cor. 1:2 TEV). In the same vein Thomas Campbell, one of the nineteenth-century Disciples founders, defined the church as "consisting of all those in every place that profess their faith in Christ and give obedience to him in all things according to the scriptures, and that manifest the same by their tempers and conduct."[1]

Unfortunately, in the course of church history, specific points of "peculiarity" became divisive. Groups claiming special insights or clinging to particular practices separated themselves. True to their understanding of the New Testament, the early Disciples fathers considered such schisms in the body of Christ evil and scandalous. To Thomas Campbell, for example, the oneness of the church was no mere object of wistful longing. The church, he declared, is by the creation of God "essentially, intentionally and constitutionally one."[2]

Desire for Oneness

An important plank in the Disciples' founding platform was that church unity could be achieved through the "restoration of primitive Christianity." Creeds, while accepted as tools for study and testimonies of faith, were rejected as bases for church definitions or membership. The New Testament was claimed as the sole authority for the ordering of church life, and all of its practices and expressions. It was believed that by simply reading the New Testament, Christians could discover the basis for common belief and practice. The hope

---

1. *Declaration and Address of the Christian Association of Washington County, Washington, Pa.* (1908), Prop. 1. Excerpts are quoted and sources of the text are cited in Lester G. McAllister and William E. Tucker, *Journey in Faith: A History of the Christian Church (Disciples of Christ).* The Bethany Press, 1975, chap. 5.
2. *Ibid.*

was that Disciples would provide sparks igniting fires of union until the church, burning bright in oneness, would shed its light into the world. In the beginning, it appeared so simple. As time continued, it became so complex.

For years, Disciples steadfastly refused to acquiesce to being labeled a "denomination." But as W. E. Garrison reminded us years ago, "Whatever they might call themselves and for however good a reason, Disciples of Christ actually did become a denomination as soon as they became a recognizably distinct group with a name by which they could be denominated."[3] He called upon the Disciples to "become increasingly a strong body of devoted and intelligent Christians, carrying their share of the common responsibility that rests upon all Christians,"[4] always prepared at the proper moment to "sink into union with the Body of Christ at large."[5]

Our hope is that we have not, nor ever will become captive of a "denominational mentality." We keep reminding ourselves and others that what makes the church peculiar is not that which distinguishes Christians from one another, but that which distinguishes Christians from the world.

Still, the church is more than just a peculiar people with a common commitment: *the church is people who have responded to a particular act of God in history.* God created the church. It still is being formed and reformed as persons respond to God's act in history in the Christ-event—his life, his death, his resurrection.

We are prone to talk about "my church" or "our church" as though it belongs to us. But that's a slip that belies our best understanding. We who compose its membership "belong" to the church and its maker. The church is not merely a product of persons—a sort of social club or fraternal organization. It is the result of divine intention.

Nevertheless, the church inevitably and pragmatically takes on forms devised by humankind.

Some early Disciples leaders overlooked the fact that the apostles and other saints who shaped the primitive church were human beings too. Unwary restorationists fell into various traps of their own making. They implied the existence of a blueprint for church structure in the New Testament. Some were certain they had found a single pattern of church organization—a radical congregationalism which recognized the autonomy of the local congregation only.

To Alexander Campbell, son of Thomas and a powerful influence, such radical autonomy was a betrayal of the wholeness of the church. As Robert L. Friedly aptly pointed out:

> Campbell felt it wrong to place in the local congregation authority that belonged to the whole church. He believed the very absence in the New Testament of detail as to church structure was intended to permit the church to establish what authority time and circumstances demanded.[6]

---

3. W. E. Garrison, *Heritage and Destiny.* The Bethany Press, 1961, p. 86.
4. *Ibid.,* p. 156.
5. This phrase is from "The Last Will and Testament of the Springfield Presbytery" signed by Barton W. Stone and others. The text is in McAllister and Tucker, *op. cit.,* pp. 77-79.
6. From "When Alexander Took His Lumps" Robert L. Friedly, in *The Christian,* Sept. 14, 1969. Vol. 107, No. 37. Christian Board of Publication.

Wholeness with Flexibility

For Disciples the development of a structure expressive of the wholeness and interrelatedness of the church has not occurred without struggle. Restorationism, including extreme congregationalism, produced two divisions in a denomination formed to bring about unity. Not until the decade of the sixties with the conclusion of a formal process of restructure did the restoration principle find expression in flexible terms most present-day Disciples consider true to the New Testament:

> The nature of the church, given by Christ, remains constant through the generations; yet in faithfulness to its mission it continues to adapt its structures to the needs and patterns of a changing world.[7]

The church is both divine in intention and human in organization.

Still, the church is more than just a peculiar group of people who have responded to a particular act of God in human history: *the church is a people called to fulfill a purpose.*

The Pauline term, "the body of Christ" (1 Cor. 12:12-31, *et al.*), probably is the scriptural image of the church most meaningful to Disciples. It gets at the matter of purpose. The church is the living body of Christ. This means that each generation of the church is to become the contemporary incarnation. The witness, nurture, and service of the church are to be keyed to the life and ministry of Christ.

Though it is a single body, the church has many parts, each of which has its own ministry (functions, gifts). "He appointed some to be apostles, others to be prophets, others to be evangelists, others to be pastors and teachers" (Eph. 4:11 TEV). Just as the analogy suggests, the church can function effectively only when all of the parts are complementing one another and fulfilling wholeness of ministry.

In its wholeness, the church is inclusive in membership and universal in its reach. "For by one Spirit we were all baptized into one body—Jews or Greeks, slaves or free—and all were made to drink of one Spirit" (1 Cor. 12:13). There are Christians on six continents. Nationality and other differences are beside the point when it comes to the church's reason for being—to carry out God's reconciling ministry.

In the midst of the mundane and pedestrian, as well as the exciting and prophetic activities of the church, there always is present a mystery which cannot be fully fathomed or completely experienced. The church in its human expression is transcended by deeper realities which ordain its destiny. It always is pointing to a goal which is only partially realized at this point in history: God's kingdom come in fullness on earth as it is in heaven.

While we Disciples can trace our heritage back through our forefathers, Barton W. Stone and the Campbells, and while we can claim identity with certain

---

7. "Preamble," *A Provisional Design for the Christian Church (Disciples of Christ).* This document or its successor is available from the General Office of the Christian Church, P.O. Box 1986, Indianapolis, Ind. 46206.

teachings of the reformers throughout church history, it all stems from Christ. In him we find our life. From him we receive our marching orders. Through him we define our future. He is the head of his continuing, living body, the church.

Power of God's Spirit

Still, the church is more than just a peculiar people responsive to a particular act of God in history and shaped by a specific purpose: *the church is people endowed with a special power.* When the church came into being, God gave it life by imbuing it with his Spirit. So the vitality of the body comes from the power of God who brought Christ forth from the dead and whose Spirit accompanies the church now.

We Disciples always have held that humankind must do for itself everything possible to meet problems and shape the future. God is not pictured as the "answer man" or the "instant problem solver." At the same time, we have been acutely aware of our need for God's power and presence to refine, ennoble, and enhance the ministries we seek to perform.

Still, while the church is people, it is not persons in isolation: *the church is that structured fellowship through which the person, purpose, and power of God are focused in human history.* Currently the Christian Church (Disciples of Christ) is structured in what we call three "manifestations"—the congregation, the region, and the general organization. In geographical terms, the congregation is local; the region is comprised of a state, part of a state, or more than one state (Canada is a region); and the general manifestation embraces the United States and Canada.

While we are familiar with the congregation, most of us are hazy about the region and the general expression.

A region exists for mission and nurture. It seeks to assist congregations and ministers; to provide opportunities for fellowship, worship, and consideration of matters of mutual concern; to lead in meeting human needs; and to help relate congregations and the general units as a functioning whole.

The general manifestation includes administrative units established for broad areas of work, central administrative functions, and specialized services. These units serve in such varied fields as homeland and overseas ministries, pensions, publishing, ecumenical affairs, higher education, fund-raising, financing of facilities, and communication.

We Disciples believe it is wrong to speak of these manifestations of the church as "levels," though we sometimes err and use that term. No part is "higher than" or "over" the other parts. There is no top or bottom, no pyramid of authority. Our preferred organizational chart consists of three circles labeled "congregation," "region," and "general," themselves linked by a larger circle symbolizing both the equality and the interdependence of these expressions of the church. Among patterns of church organization, this design of the Christian Church is unique.[8]

---

8. The three manifestations of the Christian Church (Disciples of Christ) are described in *A Provisional Design, ibid.*

In the last decade "covenant" has taken on special meaning for Disciples as we have moved from a loosely knit fellowship of congregations, associations, and agencies to a more churchly expression and structure. While each manifestation is understood to have its own authority and integrity, each also has responsibility to and for the others. "Covenant" is the word we Disciples use to express this voluntary relationship in which we are bound to God and one another.

Your response may well be "I've never seen or experienced a church such as you've described!" And you will be right. For the church of Jesus Christ is composed of people who have not yet achieved perfection. But this does not deny the seeming impossibility becoming possibility, for the church is pilgrim people who in obedience to the lordship of Christ are always in the process of becoming.

William C. Howland, Jr. is minister of National City Christian Church in Washington, D.C.

Before he assumed that pastorate in 1977, Dr. Howland served for three years as a deputy general minister and president of the Christian Church.

Across the previous two decades, he was pastor of congregations in Huntsville, Alabama; Hot Springs and Fort Smith, Arkansas; and Longview and Austin, Texas.

A native of Oklahoma, Dr. Howland earned a B.A. degree from Phillips University and a B.D. degree from Yale University Divinity School. Texas Christian University awarded him an honorary doctor of divinity degree.

Dr. Howland has held offices in Christian Church regional organizations, has served on the church's General Board and its Administrative Committee, and has been a member of the Disciples' Board of Higher Education. He has represented Disciples in various ecumenical bodies including the Texas Conference of Churches and the National Council of Churches.

The New Testament is our guide

Robert E. Gartman

She was known to the adult class where she taught as a "great Bible student" because she buttressed all her arguments with a scriptural text. The minister, a man of more liberal views, seldom punctuated his sermons with "The Bible says. . . ." During one sermon the woman became so outraged that she interrupted to demand, "When are you going to preach the Bible?" He replied, "The Bible says, 'Let your women keep silence in the churches.' If you'll practice what it says, I'll preach what it means!"

That blatant but "scriptural" male put-down only sharpens the message from this incident: Not even those of us who believe that the Bible is important are in complete agreement about how the book should be used. There is no official Christian Church position regarding the Scriptures—unless we count the oft-repeated claim that we are a "Bible people." Ingrained in most of us Disciples, though, is the belief that the Bible, particularly the New Testament, should be our guide for faith and life.

The movement that was to become the Christian Church was only about twenty-five years old when one of its founders, Alexander Campbell, released a book, *The Christian System*, summarizing his understanding of what the Bible teaches. He said, "The Bible is to the intellectual and moral world of man what the sun is to the planets and our system—the fountain and source of light and life, spiritual and eternal."[1] It was not Campbell's intention in 1835 to settle all questions for all Christians for all time with one book. To the contrary, the position of Campbell and his fellow "reformers" was that no book should take the place of study of the Bible by each Christian. Almost a century and a half later, the need still is for us to become serious students of the primary sourcebook of our faith and life as Christians.

Despite the diversity of the origins, writers, and literary forms of the materials contained in this "library," the Bible has unity. The thread connecting Genesis, Isaiah, Mark, and the Letters to the Corinthians is a story—the revelation of God in human history. One of our contemporary biblical scholars, William R. Baird Jr., identifies that story of the Bible as "the history of salvation, the record of God's dealing with men."[2]

The Old Testament is the history of ancient Israel—not just what happened, but the Hebrews' interpretation of the meaning of their life from their roots in pre-history through slavery, deliverance, the conquest of the promised land, and their cycles of turning from and returning to God. It contains their law which became the basis for law in many nations. It includes Israel's book of prayer which has become the prayerbook for synagogue, church, and the solitary seeker. It presents the prophets of Israel—not so much, as some suppose, *fore*tellers of the future as *forth*tellers speaking for God on behalf of the poor and oppressed. The Old Testament was the scriptures of the people from whom Jesus came, and for almost 2,000 years has belonged to Christians as well as Jews.

Witness to Central Event

But Christians read the Old Testament in the light of their special scriptures, the New Testament. Formed within the church, the New Testament records the early Christian community's testimony about and response to the central event of history, God's act in Jesus Christ. For a generation the words and deeds of Jesus were remembered and preserved orally. Then, as those who had known him in the flesh became few, the church in various regions produced the written Gospels. These, together with the epistles by Paul and the others, were collected into a canon of twenty-seven "books." These were selected from the mass of early Christian writings because they were believed to have come from apostles (those closest to Jesus) or were judged true to apostolic tradition.

We Disciples believe that God is able to speak anew to each generation

---

1. Alexander Campbell, *The Christian System*. Christian Publishing Co., 2d ed. of 1839, p. 15.
2. William R. Baird Jr., "The Place of the New Testament in the Church," *The Reconstruction of Theology*, ed. Ralph G. Wilburn, Vol. II of *The Renewal of Church: The Panel of Scholars Reports*. The Bethany Press, 1963, p. 82.

through the Bible. Whereas some call the Bible the "word of God," we are more inclined to say that the word of God comes to us *through* the Bible. Of course, for us as Christians the supreme revelation is Jesus Christ himself—the Word of God (John 1:1-14). We read all scripture, and examine all traditions and interpret all of our experiences in light of Jesus Christ. The really significant thing about the New Testament is that it is the authoritative record we can use in checking whether the one we experience as the Christ is the Christ in whom God spoke in Galilee, Jerusalem, and thence to the world through his apostles.

Across the centuries the church developed its traditions, doctrines, and practices. Again and again, the New Testament has served as the inspiration and guide for reformation. In the sixteenth century, Luther contended for the primacy or authority of the Bible against that of bishops and councils. In that same century, Calvin shaped reformed theology, basing it on a profound exposition of scripture. Calvinism provided the nineteenth century religious culture in which Barton W. Stone, Thomas and Alexander Campbell, and their companions in faith launched an effort to unite Christians by restoring the church as it is described in the New Testament. As Alexander Campbell stated their position, it was to "take the Bible, the whole Bible, and nothing but the Bible as the foundation of all Christian union and communion."[3]

Acts seems to have been given special attention by the Campbells, Stone, and their followers. It was from that book that the names "Christian" and "Disciples" came. The example of the early church, reported in Acts, was followed in regard to baptism, the Lord's Supper, and Sunday worship.

Notwithstanding the best of intentions and a plan that had much appeal, the Campbell-Stone movement actually added to the divisions within Christianity. The two divisive controversies in our history have been occasioned by differing views about the Bible.

Those who became the Churches of Christ thought of the New Testament as a blueprint, an absolute pattern for church organization and practices. They would permit only what is commanded. We who became the Christian Church took a broader view of the New Testament, permitting whatever is not forbidden and tolerating more freedom in interpretation. We made a slogan of a classic phrase of Rupertus Meldenius: "In essentials, unity; in nonessentials, liberty; in all things, charity." The problem, of course, was to define the essentials. For the most part, we moved away from prooftext use of scriptures with its literalism and legalism to study to discern the message of the New Testament.

Biblical Scholarship

As we entered the twentieth century, together with Christians of other denominations, we had to come to terms with the biblical scholarship of the day. The Bible was being subjected to critical examination with respect to the meaning of inspiration, the history of the text, and the supposed conflicts between the Bible and science. Our brethren who became what we call "independents" reacted to the new scholarship. Largely to protect themselves from its influences, they established their own Bible colleges. We Disciples were

3. *Op. cit.*, A. Campbell, p. 12.

more hospitable to scientific inquiries and to the developing biblical scholarship. We believed, and still do believe that the Bible can stand the most rigorous scrutiny.

We remember that Alexander Campbell believed that the same rules of interpretation should apply to the Bible as to any other writing.[4] He urged that "on opening any book in the sacred scriptures" we "consider first the historical circumstances" of the materials: Who is the author? To whom does he write? For what purpose? In what situation? When?

If there is any belief characteristic of Disciples, it is that individual Christians and congregations are free to follow truth wherever it may lead. Were we to have an official doctrine of the authority of the Bible or an official interpretation of scriptures, then *our* beliefs, the formulations of a particular generation in a certain place, would be elevated to the place of authority which belongs to God. Under the guidance of the Spirit of God, new light can break forth to us and to our children.

Well-intentioned Christians sometimes have problems understanding the Bible.

Some, for example, try to make the Bible their textbook for science, or set the Bible and science in opposition. But that is a misuse of the Scriptures. Howard E. Short describes the Bible as "a religious book . . . not a universal book of knowledge beyond which there is nothing written which is worth knowing."[5] If God is truth, then all truth is his whether in the Bible, nature, or reason.

Literalists can misconstrue scientific information as well as the message of the Bible. When I lived in the oil country of West Texas, a geologist told me of being asked by a rancher how old a certain outcropping of rock was. He replied, "Fifty million years." The rancher said, "Nope, it's fifty million and three years old." It seems that three years earlier another geologist had given the rancher the fifty-million-year figure.

There are those who have difficulty appreciating the supernatural events reported in the Bible. It is appropriate that we should seek explanations and verifications for miracles, whether ancient or modern. Still, we do well to remember that our knowledge, even in this age of amazing technology, is limited.

Many seek in scriptures to find clues to the future. Some even have devised from the Bible timetables leading to "doomsday." At least two words of caution are in order. Books like Revelation reflect the situation and hopes of the people at the time of writing: they can be better understood in reference to their time than to ours. We ought to remember how often those who have made predictions have been wrong. Besides, Jesus himself counseled against false prophets (Mark 13:22) and preoccupation with times and seasons (Acts 1:7).

Apparently even in the early church, differences of interpretation arose. Timothy was urged to "avoid disputing about words, which does no good, but

---

4. Campbell's rules for interpreting the Bible are presented on pp.16-19 of *The Christian System, op. cit.*

5. Howard E. Short, *Doctrine and Thought of the Disciples of Christ.* Christian Board of Publication, 1951, p. 13.

only ruins the hearers. Do your best to present yourself to God as one approved, a workman who has no need to be ashamed, rightly handling the word of truth. . . . Have nothing to do with stupid, senseless controversies" (2 Tim. 2:14-15, 23).

Some controversies could be avoided if we would accept the fact that not every word of the Bible is equally inspired. This is evident from Paul's own admission that in some things he had no word from the Lord but only gave his opinion (1 Cor. 7:25 ff.).

Nor should everything in the Bible be taken literally. My grandfather was a gentle and kind man who spent much of his time in his later years reading the Bible. At age 97, Grandpa became rather troubled by St. Paul's words: "If thine enemy hunger, feed him; if he thirst, give him drink: for in so doing thou shalt heap coals of fire on his head" (Rom. 12:20 KJV). Literalist that he was, Grandpa felt a dilemma. He wanted to do good even to enemies, and he was horrified at the thought of heaping coals on another's head. Taken too literally, words can lead to conclusions opposite to what is intended.

Whoever really wants to benefit from Bible study will bring to that study a desire to understand, good reasoning abilities, and the patience to use the many translations, commentaries, dictionaries, and other exegetical tools available. These are exciting times for serious Bible study.

Where once the difficulty in Bible study was a lack of any help other than the common translation (usually the King James Version), now our difficulty may be in having too many translations, commentaries, and writings which can be substituted for our own best thinking.

Something to be remembered in choosing a translation: The best are those made by panels of scholars. Joint endeavors are more likely to ensure that the most likely original language has been translated and that the theological position of a translator has not determined choices of words.

In most of our congregations, the Revised Standard Version has come to be the one most used in worship. Because of its beauty and familiarity the King James Version remains popular too. Translations such as the *New English Bible* and Today's English Version also are receiving general acceptance. Paraphrases such as *The Living Bible* may be helpful in study but should be used with caution because, in a sense, a paraphrase is as much a commentary as a translation.

In choosing commentaries, dictionaries, introductions, and other helps for Bible study, a student should take into account who the authors are. It obviously will make a difference what a writer believes about the Bible. It also makes a difference whether the writer has been scholar enough to consider all possible reasonable interpretations or is advocating his particular conclusions.

For several years I was a volunteer chaplain in the Dallas (Texas) County Jail. My success was not noteworthy. For a few weeks, though, I did think I was making a convert. A prisoner asked questions about the Bible, and for some weeks we discussed, with many listeners, the fine points of interpretation. He became familiar with the differences and likenesses of the synoptics (Matthew, Mark, Luke). I was very proud of my student. Then one day I learned that he had been confined to solitary. It seems that all the while he was my student, he and a strong-arm protégé had been charging other prisoners for "room and board" and other necessities and privileges. It isn't enough to know what the Bible says.

The Bible exists not that we should be its students or have discussions as to its authority and meaning. It was given to be our guide to faith and daily living!

Robert E. Gartman has been pastor to South Street Christian Church, Springfield, Missouri, since 1972. One of the historic Disciples congregations, South Street traces itself through the original Springfield First Christian to 1836.

A native of Port Arthur, Texas, he received B.A. and B.D. degrees from Phillips University. He earned an STM at Yale University Divinity School and is working toward a D.Min. degree at Texas Christian University.

From 1955 to 1958, Mr. Gartman was assistant to Pastor Hallie Gantz in First Christian Church, Tulsa, Oklahoma. He was minister of Urbandale Christian Church, Dallas, Texas, 1959-62, then for 10 years served Memorial Christian Church, Midland, Texas.

Mr. Gartman has served on many Christian Church boards and committees from district through general manifestation. He also has been active in various ecumenical programs.

Salvation is life renewed by love

Forrest D. Haggard

I had finished a sermon based on Phil. 3:14, "So I run straight toward the goal in order to win the prize, which is God's call through Christ Jesus to the life above" (TEV), and was standing at the door with all the greeting and meeting going on when one of my elders came up. "Forrest," he said, "I was running alright, but the wrong way, when God grabbed hold of me and turned me right around. That was before I knew the Lord and I just praise his name that the preacher down at the jail had guts enough to keep coming after me. If it hadn't been for that, I'd be a bum down at the Helping Hand Mission and not one of your fine, upstanding, well-to-do members!" To many of us, salvation is far more than a theological term.

Most of those I surveyed to get input for this chapter felt that salvation was both *goal* and *gift,* as well as the *process* of attaining or receiving. I did do a survey. It seemed to me best to ask Disciples themselves what they believe. So I surveyed both pastors and lay members of congregations in the greater Kansas City area. What follows is really a presentation of their responses and comments on "What do members of the Christian Church believe about salvation?"

Salvation seems to be the keystone of a multitude of component parts that form the archway of the Christian faith and life. Although grossly misunderstood and often associated with the theatrics and burlesque of religious fanatics, it nevertheless is the real heart and soul of Disciples thought and doctrine.

In its purest form, salvation means "made whole." To the women who touched his garment in the crowd, our Lord responded by saying, "Daughter, thy faith hath made thee whole [saved you]" (Mark 5:34 KJV). And to the sinful woman of the city who anointed his feet, Jesus said, "Your faith has saved you" (Luke 7:50).

Still, salvation is more than being made healthy (whole). It is a continuing process that involves every bit of life. Salvation is being "born again." We become members of God's immediate family. We move from being citizens of this earth only to have citizenship in a heavenly kingdom. We no longer live in darkness but in the light. We become the salt and light of the world. It is assumed that we will become productive and fruitful. We have a ministry to leave the world a better place than it was. All of this begins with a process of faith and obedience, and in the New Testament church baptism was an indispensable part of that process.

Salvation is understood to originate in the natures of God and Christ. The term "Savior" is used to describe God the Father, but especially Jesus Christ. Their salvation is from immediate or future physical danger such as in times of distress, illness, famine or war, but also from spiritual lostness (Luke 19:9, e.g.). With God, the term seems to be used for salvation from evil or danger, but with Christ it is for salvation from the power of sin or evil or death. Many Disciples have strong feelings that salvation is God's eternal purpose, and they link up the Christian Church's historical aim of promoting unity:

> God did what he had purposed, and made known to us the secret plan he had already decided to complete by means of Christ. This plan, which he will complete when the time is right, is to bring all creation together, everything in heaven and on earth, with Christ as head. (Eph. 1:9-10 TEV.)

However the word is used in Old or New Testament and however it is interpreted (literally, physically or spiritually), both clergy and laity participating in my survey agreed that "salvation is the sum and substance of the Christian faith."

Many Meanings

"Salvation" means different things to different people.

Recently I counseled a youth who some years ago went on a retreat sponsored by a fundamentalistic youth organization for Christ. While at camp, this young person was traumatized by being caught up in a dramatic presentation of what happens to a family if not all of the members are "saved": The "saved" are taken up into heaven and the "unsaved" await a bus which transports them to hell. In that same retreat, a movie was shown that depicted the "last day of judgment." This fine, sensitive child was almost destroyed by that concept of salvation.

One Sunday afternoon I had a baptismal service for a youth. During that ceremony and in the Communion service that followed, the father of this family felt moved by the Holy Spirit. It was a deeply emotional experience and effected a radical change in his life-style. That man dates his salvation from that moment. He has continued with a quiet but powerful witness in both words and life.

Sunday after Sunday, new participants are received and introduced during one of our services. Many of them respond to the open invitation to speak and to express what is on their hearts and minds. Often they use various forms of the term "salvation," saying they want, need, or have received it.

In the middle of our Bible study group meetings one Sunday evening, the receptionist brought a couple to my office and said, "These folks have a question." We introduced ourselves and I asked, "What may I do for you?" They replied, "We want to be saved." Do you have an image of "what kind of people" those folks were? Before you speak it out loud, let me tell you: They were highly educated professionals, materially successful, in their late thirties, and very articulate. They quickly revealed their hunger and their need to be "made whole." No single shattering event had driven them to a church, but rather an accumulation of events and discussions had culminated in their common understanding of a desperate need. They had no real church background. They had been prompted and nudged by some of the multitude of religious programs on the mass media. They simply had climbed into their automobile and stopped at the first church building where the lights were on and the doors were open!

Indicative of the diversity of concepts of "salvation" was the outcome of my use of a questionnaire with a large number of lay members of my own congregation. This was separate from the main survey—something extra. I wrote a series of definitions of salvation and asked the people to choose the ones they felt best represented the doctrine and thought of members of the Christian Church. Their choices included the following:

- Salvation is a gift of God.
- The individual is moved by the Holy Spirit working through the word (the gospel, either written or lived out as a witness) to receive Christ as a personal Savior.
- Salvation is the message of the love of God.
- This gift of love heals the division between humans and God.
- It is shown and continued by acts of worship such as Communion and baptism.
- This new life begins right now and continues in the life beyond.

- The person who is saved not only has new relationships right here and now but has hope of a new age where all pain, sorrow, disease, and hurt are gone.
- Salvation is a gift received in humility and concern (almost fear) rather than with feeliings of superiority and comfortableness.
- It is the "promise," the "inheritance" that belongs to us as children of God.

For the broader survey, I chose an equal number of persons from laity and clergy (seventy-five of each). It was interesting that we received an equal number of replies from the two groups and that responses from each group fell into approximately the same categories in equal amounts.

Sharing the Personal

Only one response came back unsigned and it said, "Salvation is a very personal thing between myself and Jesus Christ and is none of your business!" I would agree with the first half of that comment, but most of the Christian Church members surveyed had a definite feeling that salvation, though very personal, is to be shared. Most would understand what Paul said to the Corinthians:

> When anyone is joined to Christ, he is a new being; the old is gone, the new has come. All this is done by God, who through Christ changed us from enemies into his friends, and gave us the task of making others his friends also. (2 Cor. 5:17-18 TEV).

Some statements were quite involved, well thought-out, and documented by scriptures. Examples: "Salvation is redemption." "We are redeemed (re-purchased) by God after having pawned our life to evil." "Salvation is being bought back into the family by the blood of Christ." "Salvation is being made a whole person." "I was united inside myself after I had accepted Christ." "Salvation means that we have discontinued jumping on our horses and riding off in all directions and have found the peace, harmony, and completeness that God intended for us." "When Christ came into my life, I was delivered from sin; I mean I was a new and different person." "Salvation is putting it all together into one whole and healthy being."

Respondents had real difficulty in separating the *definition* of salvation from the *process* by which it seems to be obtained. Approximately 40 percent said that salvation could not be defined but the "way" by which it is gained could be easily understood. No matter how many steps each outlined process contained, all included one item: "Salvation is through faith in Jesus Christ as the Son of God (divine, personal Savior, God's Son, Lord of Lords, Son of the living God)."

Many others listed steps they considered necessary such as confession of sins, repentance, accepting and learning the teachings of Christ, and living the Christian life ("letting Jesus run your life" was a common way of stating this).

Even those who felt they had "always been a Christian" mentioned some process or steps by which they were made aware of the power of God in their lives. For most of these the "small group" was a key factor, and the process always included a return to or beginning of serious Bible study and personal prayer.

There is no doubt that conversion is a part of the process of salvation. In 1956, The Bethany Press published a book, *What We Believe.* Though none of the thirteen chapters is headed "Salvation," one by Charles F. Kemp is on "Conversion," and salvation and conversion are so intertwined that it is difficult, if not impossible, to separate them. Conversion is not reserved for those who have developed life-styles totally foreign to the Christian way of life. Those totally immersed in the Christian faith from the time of birth can experience a realization of conversion too. Repentance, in the purest sense of its definition, and conversion are, it seems to me, necessary ingredients for salvation. In a way, they open the door of the human life so that God's gift may be received.

Surprising to me was the fact that those I surveyed did not include baptism as part of the process of salvation. Only two even mentioned baptism, and then in connection with their view that salvation is a "gift" of God and we are "baptized in his Spirit." Certainly, in all of the congregations sampled the physical act of baptism by immersion is preached and practiced.

"Gift of God"

One whole group of respondents did not deal with the way salvation could be "earned" or attained, but rather defined what is to be received as a result. Most of these used the word "gift," e.g., "Salvation is the gift of God." They went on to define this gift as "eternal life," or "forgiveness of sins," or "freedom from sin," or "purpose and meaning for this life (a reason for living today)."

A composite of the feelings expressed would say that although salvation is a gift of God, it still is a personal responsibility of the individual to initiate the process either for himself/herself or for others through encouragement and witnessing.

About 20 percent of those who replied put together the "how" and the "what." They connected personal faith in Jesus Christ with the result of receiving a gift from God.

I have some observations about the survey itself. It seems to say that "salvation" is a meaningful word and a current issue because the responses were immediate. I received a 75 percent return on my mailings even though I did *not* include a prepaid return envelope. Lay people were as apt to "speak their piece" as were the clergy.

In most cases, both clergy and laity responded, "Salvation *to me* is. . . ." That style of personal witnessing was dominant.

Clergy respondents showed some difficulty in dealing with the "how" and "what" of salvation. The "five-finger exercise" of the pioneer Disciples evangelist, Walter Scott—"faith, repentance, baptism, remission of sins and the gift of the Holy Spirit"—evidently was out of style when the majority of these folks were in Bible college or seminary. The laity had no such difficulty. They felt that a process was important—at least they were keenly aware of the process by which they themselves were saved.

There were some common threads or elements running through all replies: *Trust* (in God, in other human beings), *doing* (moving from one life-style to another, changing habits, repenting, experiencing conversion), *growth* (Bible study, learning, prayer, service), *believing* (renewal of study of New Testament doctrine and thought) and *accepting* (feeling the will of God is a factor that must be accepted).

As one very articulate and well-educated pastor replied to me, "Forrest, *salvation* is what it's all about!"

Forrest D. Haggard is administrative pastor of Overland Park Christian Church, which serves a suburb of Greater Kansas City. That congregation had 30 members meeting in a theater when he became its minister in 1953, and it now conducts three identical Sunday morning services with an average attendance of 1,200 and has a paid staff of twenty-four.

Long involved in local, regional, and national church organizations, Dr. Haggard is president of the World Convention of Churches of Christ (Christian Church/Disciples of Christ) through its 1980 Honolulu assembly. He is a former president of the Disciples' National Evangelistic Association and has served as chairman of the board of the Graduate Seminary of Phillips University.

Dr. Haggard has served as grand master of Masons in Kansas and received the Red Cross of Constantine and thirty-third degree. He also has served as president of his county Mental Health Board and is a member of Boy Scouts' National Honor Society.

Baptism means induction, rebirth, and hope

A. Houston Bowers

Mark Twain, on his first visit to Europe, took the same tour of traditional historic spots that thousands of Americans were taking in the latter part of the nineteenth century. Somewhere in France a guide took Twain to an ancient shrine in a cave. There on a roughhewn altar burned a flame. "This," his guide said in hushed tones, "is the eternal flame."

"Eternal flame, eh?" said Twain, puffing on his giant cigar.

"Yes," the guide said, "it has been burning there continuously for at least a thousand years."

"How long?" Twain asked.

"A thousand years!"

"Puff!" Twain blew it out!

Symbols? Who needs 'em? Twain's attitude toward that venerated flame represents a deep-seated feeling present-day Americans tend to have toward symbols. Who needs them? We do! We need them badly! Symbols do something for us that nothing else can, something that we modern people may very well need more than persons in earlier times.

Baptism is one of the most significant symbols within the community of faith. Even so, before we jump into our discussion of baptism, we must lay a foundation of understanding. We begin by defining what a symbol is. It is a sign that points beyond itself. It is more than an arbitrary sign, which has no particular meaning in itself. (The word "rose" is an arbitrary sign. A rose by any other name would smell as sweet.) A symbol is a sign, but it also is related to the reality it represents intrinsically. It participates in that to which it points. A symbol is concrete, but it has the strange ability to put us in touch with things that are not concrete. In fact, the Greek verb *symbállo*, from which the word "symbol" comes, means "to bring together."

A symbol brings us together with realities otherwise inaccessible to us. For instance, a four-year-old falls down and skins his knee and comes crying his heart out to his mother. She gives him a hug and then plants a kiss on the affected knee. Now, the medicinal value of that kiss is nil. Yet the effect of it is very real. For, more often than not, the tears cease and the trembling stops and the hurt is no longer. The symbolic actions of the kiss and the hug have healing powers for the child. We cannot do without symbols. And when we try, we impoverish our lives.

But is baptism only a symbol, or something more—a sacrament? Sacraments are those rites, or more precisely signs, which Christians believe convey by Christ's appointment, an unseen sanctifying grace. The classic definition of sacrament, contained in the catechism of the *Anglican Book of Common Prayer*, is "an outward and visible sign of an inward and spiritual grace."[1] In an essay written in the mid-sixties for a restudy of baptism and the Lord's Supper among Disciples, Ralph G. Wilburn offered a "clear and simple" working definition: "A sacrament is a symbolic act of the church, under the authority of Christ, in which corporate act, by means of concrete media, God acts to seal His Word of grace in our hearts through faith and we act to bear witness to our faith in Him, in His presence and before men."[2] So again, is baptism a sacrament? It fits the definition if we believe this act of washing is used by God for the same saving purpose as the original revelatory events it symbolizes—the death, burial, and resurrection of Jesus Christ.

Difficulty with "Sacrament"

Use of the word "sacrament" is difficult for some, and for good reasons.[3] Thanks to distortion of the sacramental idea by parts of the church through much of its history, the word carries connotations of "magic" that are objec-

---

1. *Anglican Book of Common Prayer*, quoted in Massey H. Shepherd, "Sacraments," *A Handbook of Christian Theology*. The World Publishing Company, 1958, p. 331. Used by permission of Collins World Publishing Co., Inc.

2. Ralph G. Wilburn, "A Theology of the Sacraments," *Mid-Stream*, Vol. V, No. 2 (Winter 1966), pp. 12-13.

3. *Ibid.*, p. 11. Wilburn explains why a number of Protestant theologians have "certain negative feelings" about "sacrament."

tionable to many. Thomas and Alexander Campbell, Disciples founders, preferred the term "ordinances," largely because they were committed to using "Bible names for Bible things" and could find "ordinance," but not "sacrament," in the Scriptures. Through the years, Disciples probably have been bothered most by the implication that participants in a sacrament are passive, bringing nothing to the rite themselves.

Baptism has come to us by way of the same Christian community that produced the authoritative record of the revelation of Jesus the Christ. Stephen J. England, in a paper written for the Disciples' *Panel of Scholars Reports*, capsules a sacramental view that he finds in the New Testament:

> In the New Testament baptism is regarded, not as something which one does for himself, but as something that is done to him. What is done is not ultimately the act of one man (the baptizer) to another (the baptized), but the act of God upon one who in faith and with willing obedience makes his response to God's offer and call.[4]

In a paper contributed to the same series of reports, the late Professor J. Philip Hyatt answers the "symbol or sacrament?" question, "When we try to let the New Testament speak for itself, it seems that we must say that in some instances, and certainly to some people in New Testament times, baptism was not merely a symbol, but had some efficacy within itself."[5]

Back to our story of the little boy with the skinned knee. When the mother bends down and kisses the knee, it is a symbolic act of love for the child. When God reaches down through an act that represents Christ and "kisses the hurt knee" of one who has come in faith, it is a sacramental act.

While I am ready to call baptism one of the two sacraments of the church (the other being the Lord's Supper), I would agree with Karl Barth that "all the activities of the church are in their way sacramental. They are activities involving signs and symbols; moreover, they are dependent for their effectiveness on certain fixed signs and symbols."[6]

Baptism has been hotly debated throughout the life of the church. It was a topic in the early church; it was of extreme importance to the fathers of the Protestant Reformation; it was debated by many around the time of our denomination's birth in the early 1800s. Within the Christian Church we have books on top of study papers, debates on top of letters to the editor, assembly resolutions on top of consultation reports concerning such questions as these: (1) Was baptism instituted by Jesus or by the early church? (2) Should we baptize in the name of Jesus or in the name of the Trinity? (3) What is the relationship of baptism to church membership? (4) Why "believer's baptism" only? (5) Who

---

4. Stephen J. England, "Toward a Theology of Baptism," *The Revival of the Churches*, ed. William Barnett Blakemore, Vol. III of *The Renewal of Church: The Panel of Scholars Reports*. The Bethany Press, 1963, p. 207.

5. J. Philip Hyatt, "The Origin and Meaning of Christian Baptism," *The Reconstruction of Theology*, ed. Ralph G. Wilburn, Vol. II of *The Renewal of Church: The Panel of Scholars Reports*, *ibid.*, p. 280.

6. Karl Barth, *The Teaching of the Church Regarding Baptism*. SCM Press, 1948, p. 16.

is qualified to baptize? (6) Since the Greek word *baptizein* in the New Testament describes the process by which a person or an object is immersed in water and then lifted up, how can sprinkling or pouring ever be substituted?

Such discussions and disputes were put in perspective by a story Jack Finegan told when he addressed the regional assembly of the Christian Church in Washington and North Idaho several years ago. It seems that Great Britain's Lloyd George was driving through North Wales with a friend when they fell into a discussion of denominational differences. Lloyd George remarked: "The church I belong to is torn with a fierce dispute. One faction says that baptism is *in* the name of the Father. The other, that it is *into* the name of the Father. I belong to one of these parties. I feel most strongly about it. I would die for it, in fact, but I forget which one it is!" As Finegan concludes, "A heritage of dispute may persist long after the relevance of the dispute."[7]

New Testament Basis

All along, our aim has been to gain a clear understanding of early Christian baptism in order to follow the practice of those who provided the sacrament's link to the Jesus of history. Study of the New Testament, then, was the basis for what became the characteristic Disciples position and practice: Baptism of believers (not infants) by immersion for remission of sins. We still contend that careful exegesis of New Testament passages brings forth baptism's richest meaning.

As with any other practice or doctrine, not all Disciples find exactly the same meaning in baptism. However, there are four perceptions of meaning that are fairly common among us and in the ecumenical church as well.

First, Disciples believe that baptism is a form of initiation. It is at once a public identification with Jesus as Lord and Savior, and induction into his living body, the church. Repentant believers apparently were "added" that way from the day of Pentecost onward (Acts 2:38, 41).

In the concrete act of baptism, an individual takes a stand for Christ. The baptized person is "in Christ" (2 Cor. 5:14-15, 17; Gal. 2:20)—a new person no longer living selfishly but for Christ, united with him and under his control. It is the disciple-Lord relationship that is openly taken on. Just as the original Twelve were called to be disciples, so we are. Baptism "seals"[8] the call of Christ and our decision to respond.

When a person is united with Christ, he or she also is joined with brothers and sisters. Christians are "individually members" of "one body in Christ" (Rom. 12:5 *et. al.*). Distinctions of race, sex, class, and so on are wiped out by baptism (Gal. 3:27f). All are the same—sinners who have found their forgiveness in Christ, aliens who have been rescued from their separation, foreigners who are now one people.

It is in this spirit that a person is welcomed into the body of Christ. Normally

---

7. Jack Finegan, "Baptism—The Teaching of the Disciples." (Lecture, 1954), p. 1. Used by permission.

8. Ralph G. Wilburn, *Mid-Stream*, p. 33. Citing sources, Wilburn says the idea of baptism as a divine "seal" goes back to the Apostolic Fathers of the second century.

we Disciples baptize in a service of the congregation rather than a private one, thereby demonstrating the mutuality of the "membership" relationship.

Second, Disciples believe that baptism needs to be understood in connection with death and resurrection, repentance and new life. The sacrament makes contemporary the acts at Golgotha and at the tomb. The once-for-all significance of the Cross is explained repeatedly (Rom. 5:8-10; John 15:13; 1 John 4:10 *et al.*). Grace was being made available to us prior to acceptance or even appreciation. In baptism the church proclaims and the believer participates in what happened on Good Friday and Easter Sunday (Rom. 6:3-5; Gal. 3:27; Col. 2:12). It is an acted parable of the death and resurrection of Christ. Alexander Campbell termed baptism "a sort of embodiment of the gospel, and a solemn expression of it all in a single act."[9]

"Newness of Life"

Third, Disciples believe that baptism is a matter of "regeneration" (Titus 3:5; John 3:3ff). Baptism is our new birth—a radically new beginning. Our past life no longer counts for anything; it is buried! We who have been buried with Christ in baptism and who now "walk in newness of life" should consider ourselves "dead to sin and alive to God in Christ Jesus" (Rom. 6:1-11). God has freed us from sin and from ourselves. We have an opportunity to become all that we might be. Our relationship with God is such that life begins to have new meaning; we have a new understanding of all that is about us and the future looks fresh. Paul put in one statement what the New Testament affirms from beginning to end, "If any one is in Christ, he is a new creation; the old has passed away; behold, the new has come" (2 Cor. 5:17).

We Disciples feel that immersion is the form of baptism that best symbolizes the death, burial, and resurrection of Christ, and our own dying to sin and rising to new life.

Baptism is not magic. While we are still damp from the act of baptism, the old self-seeking and self-consciousness will be there to trap us. The father of the Reformation, Martin Luther, when he was afraid to trust himself, would say, "*Eo baptismo, Eo baptismo* (I am baptized, I am baptized)."

Last, Disciples believe that Christian baptism is blessed by God through the gift of the Holy Spirit. Walter Scott, the nineteenth-century evangelist, used to say, enumerating the points on five fingers, "If man has *faith* to believe, will *repent* of his sins and submits to *baptism,* God will offer *forgiveness* of sins, *salvation* and the *gift of the Holy Spirit.*" Acts 19:2-6 is an account of an incident at Ephesus indicating how important the early church believed this gift to be.

What is the significance of the Holy Spirit? When Jesus was baptized by John, a dove of peace and reconciliation descended upon him; and when this same baptism came to the world on the day of Pentecost, tongues of fire rested on the people. The tongues did not come to separate, but to unite the people so that they might hear the good news of salvation in their own languages.[10] That

---

9. Alexander Campbell, *The Millennial Harbinger.* 1847, p. 251.
10. Charles L. Wyatt, "Baptism and the Spirit" (Sermon delivered at First Christian Church, Birmingham, Alabama, January 9, 1977). Used by permission.

the Holy Spirit brings unity needs to be underscored again and again. From Peter's Pentecost sermon to the frontier preaching of Alexander Campbell, Barton W. Stone and Walter Scott, the gift of the Spirit was not enjoyed or received in a state of isolation. Paul helps our understanding: "By one Spirit we were all baptized into one body . . . and all were made to drink of one Spirit" (1 Cor. 12:13). As a Disciples leader of another generation, C. C. Morrison, said, "The Holy Spirit brings man out of separation into union."

Hyatt points to the Christian hope in baptism:

> Alexander Campbell spoke of baptism as "the gospel in water," and Luther said it was "God's Word in water." Karl Barth has written: "The efficacy of baptism consists in this, that the baptized person is placed once and for all under the sign of hope."[11]

If our day needs any sign, it is a sign of hope. May our preaching, practicing and participating rest in a "baptism of hope."

A. Houston Bowers is pastor of First Christian Church in Birmingham, Alabama.

Reared in Wichita Falls, Texas, he earned a B.A. degree from Phillips University, an M.Div. degree from the Vanderbilt University Divinity School and a D.Min. degree from Louisville Presbyterian Theological Seminary.

Since his student pastorates at Hunter, Oklahoma, and La Center, Kentucky, Dr. Bowers has served First Christian Church, Earlington, Kentucky; First Christian Church, Dumas, Texas; Jeffersontown Christian Church, Louisville, Kentucky; and the Birmingham congregation.

His service to the church outside the local parish has included youth work and Reconciliation, the race and poverty program of the Christian Church.

---

11. *Ibid.*, Hyatt, p. 285.

Faith and knowledge unfold in tension

Oliver C. Schroeder Jr.

From four decades of experience as a student, a teacher, an administrator and a trustee at various educational institutions, I have come to a deep appreciation of the relationship of reason and religion, of scientific knowledge and religious faith.

I also have come to a clearer understanding of the distinctive position and practice of the Christian Church (Disciples of Christ) with regard to this relationship. We believe in a rational approach to religion, in the reasonableness of Christian faith. Perhaps no group of Christians can lay geater claim to rational thinking on the Christian faith than we; so much is this the case that non-Disciples often speak of "the 'head religion' which characterizes the Disciples as over against the 'heart religion' of sentimental appeal."[1]

---

1. W. B. Blakemore, quoted by Granville T. Walker, *Preaching in the Thought of Alexander Campbell*. The Bethany Press, 1954, p. 87.

We Disciples began with this basic approach. Barton W. Stone reacted against the extreme emotionalism at the Cane Ridge revival in 1801 by turning to a thoughtful search of the scriptures and a reasonable understanding of what they had to say about faith and salvation—which led to the publication in 1804 of the famous "Last Will and Testament of the Springfield Presbytery" and his adoption of the name "Christian."

Similarly, Alexander Campbell, from his arrival in the United States in 1809 onward, took a carefully reasoned, logical, rational approach to religious faith and practice. He had been strongly influenced during his student years in the British Isles by what is known as "British empiricism," in particular the philosophical views of John Locke, himself a product of the Enlightenment period in Western culture.[2] Campbell's views are set forth, for instance, in *The Christian System* (1835):

> One God, one system of nature, one universe. That universe is composed of innumerable systems . . . a system of systems, not only as respects the seventy-five millions of suns and their attendant planets . . . but in reference to the various systems . . . which are but component parts of every solar system, of every planet in that system, and of every organic and every inorganic mass on each planet. . . .

> One God, one moral system, one Bible. If nature be a system, religion is no less so. God is "a God of order," and that is the same as to say he is a God of system. Nature and religion, the offspring of the same supreme intelligence, bear the image of one father—twin-sisters of the same divine parentage.[3]

Associates and followers of Stone and Campbell in the nineteenth century helped to shape "the mind of Disciples of Christ" along lines which W. B. Blakemore has delineated as "reasonable, empirical, pragmatic."[4] They asked common-sense questions—"what is the evidence of the Scriptures?" And they followed the scientific method of inductive logic in providing reasonable, orderly, evidentiary answers—Walter Scott's "five-finger exercise" outlining salvation: (1) faith, (2) repentance, (3) baptism, (4) forgiveness of sins, and (5) gift of the Holy Spirit. Thus Blakemore can speak of "our 'intellectualistic' definition of faith."[5]

Our understanding of Christian faith still is that it is a product of the mind's grappling with experience and evidence. Even though we expect to learn from those who have broken spiritual trails ahead of us, faith for us Disciples is not blind assent to earlier generations' answers. And though we know that religion

---

2. The influence of Locke and the Enlightenment on the Disciples is discussed by George G. Beazley, Jr. in a volume he edited, *The Christian Church (Disciples of Christ): An Interpretative Examination in the Cultural Context.* The Bethany Press, 1973.

3. Alexander Campbell, *The Christian System.* 2nd ed., Christian Publishing Co., 1839, pp. 13-15.

4. W. B. Blakemore in *The Reformation of Tradition,* ed. Ronald E. Osborn, Vol. I of *The Renewal of Church: The Panel of Scholars Reports.* The Bethany Press, 1963, pp. 161-183.

5. *Ibid.,* p. 182.

is a matter of the heart (feelings) as well as the head (intellect), we certainly do not consider an unreasoned response to a single emotional experience to be faith. Inherited testimony and recent inspiration are data to be considered. So are other pieces of information. For us, the decisive evidence is Jesus as we meet him in the New Testament record. We are rational believers.

Creator-encouraged Search

Still, we Disciples are not confused about who is the source or author of faith. It is God, Creator of the human mind—and everything else. The Supreme Intelligence has encouraged and rewarded the human quest for religious truth as well as scientific knowledge. God provides; humanity seeks and finds. Like knowledge of the universe, religious insights still are being unfolded to open, searching minds.

In the earliest primitive societies, curious individuals studied the heavens and found order in the movements of the sun, planets, and stars. The science of astronomy was born. Discovering fire, early men and women worshiped it as a god and used it to make life more comfortable. Chemistry began. Ancient human beings learned to use a great tree limb as a lever to dislodge a rock, an early technological achievement. Physics emerged. God constantly and consistently has encouraged people to discover scientific truths, to generate new knowledge, and to use truth and knowledge as stewards of the earth.

The Creator-discoverer relationship of God and humanity is exquisitely expressed in a letter from Johannes Kepler to Galileo Galilei dated April 19, 1610. Kepler was the discoverer of laws of planetary motion: he destroyed scientific beliefs 2,000 years old. Galileo had reported to Kepler that the moon was not a smooth sphere shining by its own light: assumptions on which scientific minds had acted since the time of Aristotle were shattered. Study Kepler's response to this explosion of scientific knowledge:

> . . . I yearned to discuss with you, most accomplished Galileo, in a highly agreeable kind of discourse, the many undisclosed treasures of Jehovah the creator, which He reveals to us one after another. For who is permitted to remain silent at the news of such momentous developments? Who is not filled with a surging love of God, pouring itself copiously forth through tongue and pen?
>
> . . . I have also thought it worthwhile, in passing, to tweak the ear of the higher philosophy. Let it ponder the questions whether the almighty and provident Guardian of the human race permits anything useless and why, like an experienced steward, He opens the inner chambers of his building to us at this particular time. Such was the opinion put forward by my good friend Thomas Seget, a man of wide learning. Or does God the creator, as I replied, lead mankind, like some growing youngster gradually approaching maturity, step by step from one stage of knowledge to another? (For example, there was a period when the distinction between the planets and the fixed stars was unknown; it was quite some time before Pythagoras or Parmenides perceived that the evening star and the morning

star are the same body; the planets are not mentioned in Moses, Job, or the Psalms.) Let the higher philosophy reflect, I repeat, and glance backward to some extent. How far has the knowledge of nature progressed, how much is left, and what may the men of the future expect?

. . . In the center of the world is the sun, heart of the universe, fountain of light, source of heat, origin of life and cosmic motion. But it seems that man ought quietly to shun that royal throne. Heaven was assigned to the lord of heaven, the sun of righteousness; but earth, to the children of man. God has no body, of course, and requires no dwelling place. Yet more of the force which rules the world is revealed in the sun (in the heaven, as various passages of Scripture put it) than in all the other globes. Because man's house is otherwise, therefore, let him recognize his own wretchedness and the opulence of God. Let him acknowledge that he is not the source and origin of the world's splendor, but that he is dependent on the true source and origin thereof. . . .[6]

Kepler's epistle fuses a faithful knowledge and a knowing faith.

In our time the splitting of the atom, the walking on the moon, the using of radio and television for instantaneous worldwide communication, and the engineering of genes to yield new life forms are worthy successors to earlier advances. However, these marvelous scientific achievements do not represent the triumphs of individuals as did those of pioneers in previous centuries. Recent leaps forward have been achievements of persons organized into vast institutional systems. The process continues, now at a truly explosive rate.

Religious Growth

Religious faith has developed similarly across the centuries since antiquity. God used the children of Israel to advance religious faith by opening the people's eyes to belief in one Supreme Being. The Lord established a covenant between himself and Abraham and that patriarch's descendants, and the Hebrew people came in time to perceive that God was compassionate even when the nation was unfaithful. The Ruler of the universe promulgated moral codes to make faith a fulfilling living experience. Receiving the Ten Commandments, the Hebrew people developed an elaborate system—the Law.

"But when the time had fully come," as Paul expressed it (Gal. 4:4), "God sent forth his Son." God became flesh in Jesus to reveal himself as fully as possible to humanity and to demonstrate a living style. Humankind was to emulate Christ, follow his path, be true to his teachings. Love was to be the law controlling all relationships and channeling knowledge.

We believe that there is potential for good in all that God offers and the inquisitive, responsive human mind finds.

---

6. *Kepler's Conversation With Galileo's Sidereal Messenger, The Sources of Science,* No. 5. Johnson Reprint Corp., 1965, pp. 11-12, 40, 45.

In modern times, Albert Einstein demonstrated a capacity to match unprecedented scientific knowledge with the deepest of religious convictions. A person with unbounded humanity, he *knew* God existed. He reverently proclaimed from his knowledege, "I shall never believe that God plays dice with the world."[7] The scientist observed that all is orderly and acknowledged God as Creator of that supreme order. Einstein noted that "God is subtle but not malicious" in dealing with his creation.[8] "God loves," Einstein affirmed, and that is why he abhorred war, hypocrisy, dogma, and cruelty. His life enmeshed scientific education with religious experience.

Today, humanity confronts a challenge of crucial proportions—keeping scientific knowledge in creative balance with religious faith. It was almost thirty years ago that Einstein warned of the danger of nuclear war and the possible annihilation of the human family. Buckminster Fuller recently stated:

> Humanity has come to an extraordinary moment. We have the option to survive, but it is absolutely touch and go. The question is whether the human family can begin to realize: *We are here for our minds.* At this point in time the fist and muscle control humanity. If the fist stays around for the next ten years, we're all through, wiped out. If we get through the next ten years with mind in control, we'll make it. You might call the next decade Earth's final examination period.[9]

Are we now as God's trustees to betray our trust? Are we to destroy ourselves and our planet, or are we to preserve the living fauna and flora over which we have been given dominion? Shown forbidden fruit, will we pick it?

Opportunities from God

In periods of great scientific triumphs, God presents opportunities for deeper religious commitments. One of the finest expressions of this matching of knowledge with faith occurred during the fifteenth and sixteenth centuries. Copernicus discovered that the earth revolved around the sun, and from that the concept of the solar system began. Gutenberg invented printing from movable type, and wider dissemination of knowledge became possible. Columbus explored the great unknown sea to the west and others rounded the Cape of Good Hope, starting the final conquest of planet earth. Simultaneously, a number of movements began slicing through the complex and abusive traditions of the medieval church to the New Testament. Luther in Germany, Zwingli in Zurich, Calvin in Geneva and others ignited a higher faith. Christians would approach God personally through the open Bible, faith, and commitment. Humanity had countered the new science and technology with an explosion in the realm of faith—the Protestant Reformation.

7. Philipp Frank, *Einstein, His Life and Times.* Alfred A. Knopf, Inc., 1947. Quoted in John Bartlett, *Familiar Quotations,* 14th ed. Little, Brown & Co., 1968, p. 950, quoting Albert Einstein. Used by permission.

8. Rudolph Flesch, *New Book of Unusual Quotations.* Harper & Row, 1957, p. 138, quoting Albert Einstein.

9. "Journey Into the Inner Space of Buckminster Fuller" by Stewart Dill McBride. *Christian Science Monitor,* March 9, 1977. pp. 14-15. Used by permission.

God has given us another opportunity, larger and more dangerous than earlier ones. The need is for individuals so firmly based in the way of Jesus that they will be prepared to manage the gigantic scientific advances of the years just ahead. Can our religious fervor and growth keep pace? Will our scientists, like Kepler, feel a "surging love of God" when modern miracles are achieved? In the excitement of discovery, will we marvel at the "opulence of God"? Is it possible for us, like Einstein, to perceive God's infinite order and understand humanity's place in it? Our beginning point is to recognize this unprecedented moment in God's history for what it is.

We Disciples of Christ—"reasonable, empirical, pragmatic" (and I would add "biblical")—are as well equipped as any other group of Christians to help humanity confront its twentieth-century challenge successfully. Much as science and education are making gains through systems and institutions, the church must rely on strong institutions in helping individuals prepare and cope. Christian higher education always has been important to us Disciples. Along with that, we must strengthen religious education in our congregations, and focus our worship and work to bring persons face to face with the hardest evidence God ever presented—Jesus of Nazareth. Not in the distant now-less-treacherous past but in the scientific Eden in which we find ourselves.

It is a responsibility of people who see God behind both scientific breakthroughs and the incarnation to till our paradise and keep it as a garden for life, not a tomb of death.

Oliver C. Schroeder Jr. is a member of the law faculty and director of the Law-Medicine Center at Case Western Reserve University in Cleveland, Ohio.

He is an elder in Euclid Avenue Christian Church in Cleveland, a director of the Christian Board of Publication, a trustee of Christian Theological Seminary, and vice-president and trustee of Cleveland Christian Home.

Deeply involved in community and social concerns, Dr. Schroeder is a councilman of Cleveland Heights, Ohio, where he was mayor in 1972-74. He is a fellow of the American Bar Foundation, a fellow of the Ohio State Bar Foundation, a member and past president of the American Academy of Forensic Sciences, and vice-president of the Forensic Sciences Foundation.

He is the author or editor of a number of books and periodicals, principally in the fields of criminal justice, medical jurisprudence, constitutional law, international law, and the legal profession.

The Lord's Supper recalls the Christ-event

William F. Loader

A relatively young elder, whom I greatly admire, told me that he had "not really thought through Communion" until after he became an elder. He regretted that. And he wondered how he had "missed out" while participating in the Lord's Supper almost every Sunday: "Maybe we assume too much. Maybe we don't discuss Communion enough . . . a lot of doing, but not enough thinking."

No one can write with authority on beliefs of Disciples of Christ. Within the Christian Church, we proudly proclaim our individual right to interpret scripture for ourselves. (That pride just might be our greatest sin.) Nonetheless, if we agree on any belief in addition to the lordship of Christ, surely it is the primacy of the Lord's Supper in the worship of the church.

Yet one young man told me that he saw the Lord's Supper as just a part of the worship service. That was it. "The sermon's longer," he said, "so it's hard to think of Communion as being more important."

Called the Eucharist (thanksgiving) by a few and Communion by most of us, the Lord's Supper is generally considered the essential part of our Sunday worship. If we don't have a minister to deliver a sermon, a lay person usually presents a message. But if a last-moment emergency leaves us without a speaker, we still expect worship to be conducted with the Lord's Supper at the heart of the service. So while its form and placement may vary, Communion is thoughtfully included within each Sunday's worship experience.

A minister normally presides at the Table, expressing the invitation to participate, often repeating Paul's caution that we first examine ourselves (1 Cor. 11:28). After the minister presents a scriptural account of Christ's actions and words in instituting the Meal, one or two elders offer prayers over the bread and the cup. It is well understood among Disciples that the Supper is the *Lord's* and that it is open to all who believe that Jesus is their personal savior. Therefore, the Communion elements are offered to all worshipers, usually on trays passed through the congregation.

We do not consider either an ordained minister or elders necessary for carrying out this sacrament. Normally ministers and elders share in administration of the Lord's Supper. But if persons holding those offices are not present, the group selects others to carry on. Disciples hold that at baptism all Christians become priests responsible for serving one another. We certainly do not think of this as carelessness with the Meal. On the contrary, we expect whoever serves at the Table to do so with reverence and sensitivity.

Our belief in the importance of the Eucharist leads some congregations to celebrate it early in the service of worship so none will miss it. Others participate in Communion midway in the service, symbolically indicating its centrality. Still others conduct the Lord's Supper at the close of the service, viewing it as the climactic moment of the worship experience. But in our sense of its significance, we Disciples feel that whenever the Lord's Supper occurs, it is first.

A young lady told me she sees the Lord's Supper as a time to separate from other times. "It's a special time," she said, "for special remembrance of Christ and all that his life tells us about God's love, and our part in it."

Focal Point

This sacramental meal is so important to Disciples that our church buildings frequently are designed to draw attention to the Communion table. Common for many years has been placement of the table at the front of the sanctuary in the center, either on a raised chancel or on the same level as most of the worshipers. In some sanctuaries, seating is arranged around three or four sides of the table so that the congregation has the feeling of actually gathering around it.

The table, then, literally is a focal point for regular spiritual renewal of the Christian's life. A ministerial student spoke to me in terms of the "unique community" at the Lord's Table. He said he felt the combined strength of others joining with him and Christ in the very center of God's love. He said he wished that he could find that same communion of spirit more often and in more places. The implication was that he couldn't.

The centrality of the Lord's Supper to Disciples dates back to our frontier beginnings. In fact, many claim our movement was born at the Table. Our forefathers could not accept a situation which prevented Christian brethren from breaking bread together merely because they belonged to differing denominations. That dissatisfaction contributed mightily to the birth of the Christian Church, where all believers are welcomed to our Lord's Table.

Most Disciples believe that the Lord's Supper is not the private preserve of any congregation or denomination. We are baffled by the audacity of Christians who still refuse to share Communion with all persons who have been baptized. We rejoice in the growing consensus that the unity of the body of Christ is denied when his followers are not united around his Table. It is depressing to hear church leaders refer to other denominations as "other communions." Such phrasing appears to dispute a position which Disciples almost universally hold: There is but one Communion.

In his book, *The Christian System*, Alexander Campbell, a founder of the Disciples movement, advocated observance of the Lord's Supper every Sunday.[1] He assembled a persuasive case by combining Acts 2:42 with Acts 20:7, "On the first day of the week, when we were gathered together to break bread . . . ." It is doubtful whether many Disciples can recite the chapter and verse numbers of those "proving" passages. And it's certain that many of us feel uneasy about Campbell's legalistic approach. Still, most of us believe that weekly Communion is scriptural.

As passing years have separated Disciples from the frontier, we have become increasingly attentive to educated opinion. This continuing growth probably has been quickened by our constantly improving church school materials. But there still is a lingering suspicion among many Disciples that some professional scholars engage in vocabulary gymnastics—the elite writing for the elite. When lay persons approach scholarly resources, we often encounter more mystery in the writing than there is in the message.

Symbols Not Mysterious

Few Disciples are troubled by mystery at the Lord's Table. We think we understand what is said when we hear that the good shepherd became the sacrificial lamb. We don't have to imagine Jesus, the carpenter, being magically transformed into a shepherd and then into a sheep. So we are not puzzled by the bread and wine symbols. We do not look for these emblems to become anything more than what they appear to be. Neither do we get hung up in the mystery of our awareness of the living presence of Christ. We may study and search for fuller meanings, but we accept in faith some things we don't understand.

Richard M. Pope, professor of church history at Lexington Theological Seminary, has written, "The full meaning of the Communion which we experience in the Lord's Supper can only be known in the hereafter, when we shall see Christ as he is, and be known even as we are known."[2] That is a splen-

1. Alexander Campbell, *The Christian System*. 2nd ed., Christian Publishing Co., 1839, pp. 321-354.

2. Richard M. Pope, "Where Two or Three Are Gathered Together: A Disciple's Interpretation of the Lord's Supper," *Mid-Stream*, Vol. V, No. 2 (Winter 1966), p. 148.

did statement of Dr. Pope's faith. And his paper, I think, is an outstanding piece for study—the purpose he intended for it. However, I believe that many thoughtful Disciples lay persons, when discussing Communion, would say that its full meaning may not be known, but what is known surely is full of meaning.

We know that scripture says that Jesus called his disciples together for supper, the last before his crucifixion. He had a special message for them (and us). After a time of eating and fellowship, he took up two very ordinary items from the table—a loaf and a cup. Then he used them as symbols in an extraordinary way to ensure that God's incredible love would be remembered. The incident, as "delivered" by Paul:

> The Lord Jesus on the night when he was betrayed took bread, and when he had given thanks, he broke it, and said, "This is my body which is for you. Do this in remembrance of me." In the same way also the cup, after supper, saying, "This cup is the new covenant in my blood. Do this, as often as you drink it, in remembrance of me." For as often as you eat this bread and drink the cup, you proclaim the Lord's death until he comes (1 Cor. 11:23b-26).

Disciples find no mystery in what Jesus did. He thanked God for the food and drink. This certainly would not be unusual. But then the unusual happened. Bread, which Jesus had used as a synonym for life in several earlier discussions with the disciples, became a *symbol* for *his* life. He thanked God for his life. Then he broke that life symbol. There can be no twisting of meaning because he called the broken bread his body. His life was given for them, he said. The bread was then passed among them for each disciple to take a piece.

Then he did much the same with the cup. But he went further. He identified the wine (cup) as a symbol of his blood. But first he said that it was a new covenant—a new pact between him and them. He poured out a promise to them. He made them a part of his death and his return. And he said more than "Do this . . . in *remembrance* of me." He said, "As often as you eat this bread and drink the cup, you *proclaim* the Lord's death *until he comes*."

He was inviting them to accept his life and his death as part of their living. And he was saying that when they drank the wine, they were *witnessing* to his death. Do this till I return, he said. And that was the new covenant. No longer would they live with a covenant between God and them based on *law*. This new relationship would be based on God's endless *love* as demonstrated by the gift of his total being—his very blood.

Now, put all of that into present tense, because we believe in a living Lord—a Lord who offers us everything that he offered those who have gone before us. Writing of himself, Paul said, "Christ . . . lives in me" (Gal. 2:20). And Jesus, praying for "those who are to believe," spoke of being "in them" (John 17:20, 23). *Christ in us*. Obviously, the material symbols are to help ready us to take part in a spiritual experience.

Living Presence

I have read a dozen scholars but have yet to understand how or why it is that I actually feel Christ with me when I join in the Lord's Supper. All I know is what the Scriptures report that Christ said, and the way that I feel. So this becomes a personal witness.

I'm convinced that my lack of openness explains why sometimes I feel nothing at the Table. Other times, I want to cry with joy in the feeling I have of his nearness. I strongly suspect that a great many Disciples share similar thoughts and feelings. Our Lord is there. It is his Supper. The symbolic elements for spiritual feasting are there. Nourishment can be found there. But the degree to which the Meal satisfies our needs pretty much depends upon us. A minister friend has confided that he sometimes feels the presence of Christ all about him at the Table. And sometimes he does not. He believes that the spirit of Christ is known according to our state of readiness.

I think the Meal's meaning can be affected by the appointed servants. Are they breaking the loaf as a cue for speaking instead of seeking? Do they lift the cup in toasting, instead of anticipation? Are they helping me to remember or are they distracting me?

An elder's prayer often has opened me to or removed me from a rich Communion experience. Some elders have driven me away from the Table with fumbling, ill-prepared prayers. Some prayers ramble all over the countryside, flitting from good weather and spring flowers to something mentioned in the day's sermon. Simply trying to follow this kind of trip is such a mental challenge that little opportunity remains for a spiritual meeting. Still, with passing years, I've concluded that to remember Christ is to be mindful of God's overwhelming love. And that includes his whole creation. So I now am almost convinced that even the wandering prayer that haphazardly plucks up unrelated bits of evidence of God's beautiful power and concern has a place at our Lord's Table. I think now that in narrowly defining what makes a suitable Communion prayer, I have at times tried to structure God's message. I, not the elder, have blocked out the spirit of Christ.

"Do this in remembrance of me," he said. Christ wants us to remember that his body—his life—is for us. A part of it for each of us. And his blood was poured out for us. That is too great a price for us to forget. But if we are to remember him, we need to go even deeper than his awesome sacrifice and recognize that until he returns, the spirit of Christ is still God among and within us.

What a gift! It defies full understanding. Wretched beings that we are. Limitless love that God is. How, even in God's mind, do we merit such a gift? We don't, of course. The living presence of Christ is a measure of God's grace.

At times I think I see fleeting glimpses of Christ in other persons. And during the Lord's Supper, I often have felt his spirit moving within me. Upon leaving the church building, that feeling sometimes continues. And I find myself hoping that people can see a little of Christ in me. I not only wish it; I pray for that.

William F. Loader is executive vice-president of T. Jefferson Wright Associates, a Louisville, Kentucky, advertising and public relations firm. Formerly he was with WHAS-TV, AM, FM, Louisville, for 25 years.

An elder and cabinet member in Louisville's First Christian Church, Mr. Loader formerly served as chairman of the board and on major functional committees in that congregation.

He is a public relations practitioner accredited by the Public Relations Society of America. Sharing his skills and experience, Mr. Loader serves on communication advisory committees of the Christian Church and the Kentucky Association of Electronic Cooperatives, and is PR advisor to Kentucky Friends of 4-H.

Mr. Loader also is a member of the board of the Kentucky unit of Recording for the Blind and the Jefferson County unit of the Kentucky Division of the American Cancer Society.

He has written numerous articles for Kentucky publications, and is a frequent speaker and panel moderator on communications for a variety of groups.

We proclaim and experience in worship

T. Garrott Benjamin, Jr.

While worship historically has been central to the life of the Christian Church (Disciples of Christ), it has not always been respected as *the* primary act of the community of faith. If we Disciples are to be obedient to Jesus Christ and joyful in his Spirit (I believe these are essentials of the faith), we must restore worship to priority status among us.

I am not suggesting that all of our congregations should worship exactly alike because Disciples get their genius from both their freedom and their diversity. In our tradition, unity does not necessarily require uniformity. Even though practices and rites are quite similar in many Disciples congregations, none of our worship services are identical—and for that we can say, "Glory hallelujah!"

"Worship" comes from the Saxon "worthship," which basically means that worship is the attitude and activity that reflects the worth of God. Obviously, with such a definition, which encompasses both personal and corporate worship, one could write not merely a chapter, but an entire book or even a series of books. But for the purposes of this chapter, we shall build on this strict definition while limiting its scope. In the main, our focus will be on congregational worship.

Personally, I can affirm this statement:

> Worship occurs where grace as the pardoning and empowering act of God in Christ and faith as the response of man meet together, resulting in adoration, reconciliation and loving obedience to Him.[1]

A simpler way of putting it is "God acts and man responds in praise" or "man's praise of God for his mighty acts and wonderful works among the children of men."[2]

Whether folk have this kind of experience alone or in a group, they begin to worship. I say "begin" because one can never really fully comprehend the acting hand of God or the responding heart of man. Each "coming together" of creature and Creator is only the beginning of understanding and not the end. So often, just when we think we understand God, he amazes us with his mystery.

Through the years, Disciples have followed a fairly uniform "order of worship." Most Sunday worship services of Christian Churches consist of hymns of praise, scripture readings, prayers, offering, sermon and the essential Communion service. But the style or "manner" (as Alexander Campbell, one of the Disciples' founders, called it) of worship has been as varied as is humanly thinkable. In light of our claim to be a "New Testament people" and given the fact that the New Testament offers no set liturgy, it is predictable that Disciples worship would have both order and diversity.

Some Disciples congregations are very formal and staid while others are rather informal and emotional. However, more and more congregations are taking a holistic view of worship (including both order and spontaneity, for example), and as a result are reaping a great harvest.

Nowadays, most Disciples worship services are planned. That is, elements of a service—hymns, readings, special music, sermon and so on—are planned to contribute to a unified experience. Many more resources, aids, and media are used in worship now than at the beginning of this century or as recently as thirty years ago. Processions, litanies, choral responses, transitional music, candles, banners, tape recordings, projected pictures, drama, interpretive dance—these indicate the range of elements that can be found in Disciples services in the late seventies. Even in congregations that encourage spontaneity, some planning of worship is done.

---

1. "Statement adapted from the report on 'Worship and Witness of the Church,' presented to the Consultation on Church Union, Oberlin, Ohio, March 19-21, 1963," quoted in *Worship in the Christian Church*, a report of a Worship Study Commission. Christian Board of Publication, 1969. p. 29.
2. As used in these definitions, "man" means "humankind" (young and old of both sexes), not "adult male." Similarly, use of masculine pronouns for God is not intended to convey gender, but the Christian concept of God as personal.

Celebration and Praise

Worship at its best is celebration and praise. These are essential ingredients of human response to the mighty acts of God. To be meaningful, worship should have the joy and enthusiasm of a holy party. True, part of our response to the Creator and Ruler of the universe should be awe—"the fear of the Lord." But one way to honor God is to rejoice in all that he has done. Wherever we find celebration and praise, there we find *life*.

In recent decades the bulk of our Disciples congregations have slipped into a cold and deadening formalism and rationalism in worship. This apparently has resulted from suspicion of any form of emotionalism. Among mainline Disciples, emotions seemingly are regarded as inferior to reason. Whether they are indeed inferior is far too subjective a speculation for me. I would rather think of emotions as real and integral to the whole. Historically, human beings were emotional before they were rational, which makes the emotions not better but at least primary.

It always has interested me how selective we are about emotional responses. When we praise human beings, we are jubilant and enthusiastic. Go to a football game and watch the forces of violence stir up the emotions, for example. Yet some of the same people who yell themselves hoarse at an athletic event come to church and bury their honest emotions. We Disciples are missing an important dimension of worship when we restrain ourselves from praising the Lord zealously and openly.

How do we achieve this joy, enthusiasm, and zeal in worship? We start by challenging some myths.

The first myth is that it doesn't matter whether worship pleases people, only whether it glorifies God. We never should circumscribe and limit our worship in such a way that we ignore the needs and longings of humanity as we praise our mighty God. Christ died for us; then certainly *we* ought to care about "us." Keith Watkins has put it this way: "Without the praise of God, church life is inconsequential and of very little power. Unless it finds favor with the people, a congregation fades away and loses even the ability to praise."[3] A holistic view is not "either-or" but "both-and." We must direct our praise to God but with the conditions, yearnings, and aspirations of human beings in mind. If God is *truly praised*, the people will be *truly pleased*.

The second myth to be challenged is that there is a conflict between the emotions and the intellect as they apply to worship. Not only is there *no* conflict but they compliment each other and give worship its wholeness. We human beings are neither cerebral nor somatic. We are both! We both think and feel. If worship is to be relevant to the whole person, then it must address both the mind and the heart of humankind.

A *whole* worship service is one in which the scripture lessons, hymns, prayers, collects, litanies, offering, Communion, and sermon both speak to the deep feelings of worshipers and stimulate their minds. Cogitation and

---

3. Keith Watkins, "Praising God—and Pleasing the People," *The Disciple*, Vol. 2, No. 21 (Nov. 2, 1975), p. 3.

celebration—without either, worship is incomplete. Maybe it is the tendency among Disciples to provide only half of a worship experience that results in half-filled sanctuaries, half-subscribed budgets and half-met needs.

Worship should not be somber, stoic, and stolid. Instead, there should be spontaneous expressions of joy—laughter, shouts, or hand-clapping. The early church was full of joy. Even the Lord's Supper is for celebration, not sadness. We are not on the dark side of the Cross but on the bright side. We are supposed to be glad, for he is risen. Every memorial need not be a funeral; but then again, are not funerals supposed to be joyful? I do not mean light-hearted. I mean filled with joy—a deep and abiding satisfaction in the "victory that overcomes the world" (1 John 5:4).

Centrality of Preaching

The third myth is that Communion is the central event of the worship service. We Disciples recognize how important the Lord's Supper is as the symbol of our best understanding of Christ. It is not possible for me to visualize a Christian Church worshiping on Sunday without gathering around the Lord's Table, but we must never confuse this meaningful observance with the primary mission of the church. It is true that in the first few years of its existence the church found the communal meal or "breaking of bread" particularly significant. But I believe that through growth in the Spirit, the apostles found that the sermon or the telling of the gospel story was of a higher (or at least equal) significance.

Preaching of the Word properly is the central event in Disciples worship. It is through the preaching of the gospel that people are saved. It is preaching that builds up the community of faith. Supper and sermon are not in competition; but when preaching is de-emphasized, there usually is decline and decay. Preaching builds and the Holy Meal nurtures and sustains.

The fourth myth is that the worship service, or more specifically, preaching is a spectator event in which the congregation listens passively while the preacher delivers a monologue. I believe that it is in the best tradition of Disciples for worship to be dialogical with pulpit and pew in active exchange, either verbal or nonverbal. If one merely listens, his or her listening should be an *active* listening. I call this process or model "participatory preaching." Reuel L. Howe indicates some valid reasons why lay people should be participants in the preaching event:

> First, they should be participants because they are part of the church, a part of the people of God! As such they are not meant to be passive recipients of, but active participants in, the witness of the church in the world.
>
> Second, they should participate because, out of the data and experiences of their lives, they produce insights and points of view that must be taken into account if there is to be any true meeting of meaning between man and God.
>
> Third, they should be participants because it is Christian belief that God speaks to men through men, especially through his people if they are open to him. If communication is two-way, then preaching should mean:

(1) communication between congregation and preacher; and (2) between members of the congregation and people with whom they live and work.[4]

The fifth myth is that preaching can have a valid base outside the Bible. The Old and New Testaments taken together—the whole Bible—is the only common book of the Christian community, our primary source of worship materials. At its best, worship is an exposition and proclamation event in which the church learns of the gospel of Christ as it is found in the Scriptures. Since Thomas Campbell uttered them in 1809, we Disciples have dutifully repeated his assertion that "where the Scriptures speak, we speak; and where the Scriptures are silent, we are silent."[5] Far too often, however, we have stumbled blindly along quoting newspapers, theological journals, voluminous authors and pastoral counselors, and then almost as an afterthought added a proof text or two from the Bible or a word about Jesus. Such preaching is without real life because it is cut off from the roots of faith.

Bible Study

Bible study encourages and strengthens worship. For example, a congregation engaged in participatory preaching sometimes helps "write" its pastor's sermons. Prior to the preaching event, the people join the minister in study of the scripture passage that will be the sermon text. Then as the preacher prepares, he or she takes into account the questions, longings, and understandings of members of the congregation. They already are "plugged in" when the service starts. The sermon is more meaningful because they helped to shape it. This does not negate the prophetic role of the preacher; it just makes him or her a more responsible prophet.

What I have proposed in the process of puncturing myths is revitalized corporate worship of a kind most of us Disciples would find meaningful. Since worship indicates the "worth" we place on God, we feel that it should have priority status in the life of the church. We would welcome more opportunities to respond to God with honest outpourings of our feelings, especially our joy over what he has done. It would be in keeping with our heritage of freedom and shared ministry for Disciples worship services to rely heavily on participation of all of the people. We long have recognized that preaching, firmly based in the Bible, is the most effective medium for bringing gathered people into life-changing confrontations with the gospel. I believe that renewal of congregational worship along these lines would be entirely in keeping with traditional thought of the Christian Church.

It is from worship that congregations get their "grow and go." A vital congregation is one able to get human beings closer to one another (inside the church), closer to their brothers and sisters (outside), and closer to God. For a short, exciting description of how irrepressible Spirit-powered life burst forth in the earliest church, read Acts 2, particularly vss. 42-47. (The Disciples' founders

---

4. From *Partners in Preaching:* Clergy and Laity in Dialogue, by Reuel L. Howe. Copyright © 1967 by The Seabury Press, Incorporated. Used by permission of the publisher. The Seabury Press, 1967, p. 43.

5. Robert Richardson, *Memoirs of Alexander Campbell,* quoted in Lester G. McAllister and William E. Tucker, *Journey in Faith: A History of the Christian Church (Disciples of Christ).* The Bethany Press, 1975, p. 110.

considered this a key passage.) Powerful preaching, devotion to authoritative teaching about Jesus, fellowship, breaking of bread, and prayer; togetherness in everything; and praise of God—these were aspects of that church's worship. "And the Lord added to their number day by day those who were being saved" (vs. 47). Almost twenty centuries later, we live in a vastly different world. But the basic formula of the early church is one that still will work for us.

T. Garrott Benjamin, Jr. is pastor of Second Christian Church, Indianapolis, Indiana, the largest predominantly black congregation of the Christian Church anywhere.

He is a former president of the Disciples' National Evangelistic Association and has served on the Christian Church's General Board and its Administrative Committee.

Dr. Benjamin is host of a weekly television series, "Livin' for the City," on WRTV Channel 6, Indianapolis, and formerly hosted another TV series for several years.

He was founding president of the United Northwest Area community organization (UNWA) in Indianapolis, and co-founder and vice-president of the Movement Against Racism for Change, Inc. (MARC), a consulting team that conducts workshops to change attitudes and combat white racism. He has addressed universities, government agencies, and church groups.

A native of St. Louis, Dr. Benjamin earned a B.S. degree from St. Louis University and M.Div. and D.Min. degrees from Christian Theological Seminary. His recognitions include Black Bicentennial Honoree for Indiana, awarded in 1975 by the Indiana Bicentennial Commission.

All believers share in Christ's ministry

Grace Riddell Ford

Whether we always act like it or not, those of us in the Christian Church understand that God calls each of us to a ministry—a ministry that is . . .

> as unique as each individual,
> as universal as the whole people of God,
> as self-giving as Christ himself.

We value professional ministers—those set apart by ordination or licensing. But we feel that as baptized Christians, each of us bears the vocation of servant (minister). As *A Provisional Design for the Christian Church (Disciples of Christ)* puts it, "By virtue of membership in the church, every Christian enters into the corporate ministry of God's people."[1]

---

1. Section VI, "Ministry," *A Provisional Design for the Christian Church (Disciples of Christ)*. This document or its successor is available from the General Office of the Christian Church, P.O. Box 1986, Indianapolis, Ind. 46206.

Because we hold a variety of gifts, the ministry we have in common finds various expressions. Because one Lord is glorified and the same commission has been given to all of us, we have a single purpose. Because of the pervasive need to transcend divisions and alienation, our ministry should express and produce reconciliation and wholeness.

Concepts of the ministry we share are derived from the Bible, both the Old Testament record of the Hebrews' spiritual pilgrimage and the New Testament testimony of the community called into existence by the ministry of Jesus. The biblical story is that of God calling people to minister, serve, reconcile in the world God created and loves.

Abraham, that 75-year-old layman, was called by God to go from his land to another with the promise that God would bless him. This was not to be an empty blessing, but one with a purpose. Because God blessed Abraham, he was to be a blessing: "and by you all the families of the earth will bless themselves" (Gen. 12:1-3). This summons by God to be a blessing in a world neighborhood speaks to us in our time.

Isaiah was another layman of unusual statesmanship and devotion. In the midst of overwhelming forces he proclaimed a servant role for the "chosen" of the sovereign God:

> "I am the Lord, I have called you in righteousness,
>   I have taken you by the hand and kept you;
> I have given you as a covenant to the people,
>   a light to the nations,
>   to open the eyes that are blind,
>   to bring out the prisoners from the dungeon,
>   from the prison those who sit in darkness" (Isa. 42:6-7).

The faithful still are called to be God's people, the *laos*, bearing the message of reconciliation in their daily lives.

This same theme permeates the New Testament. On an occasion when the disciples were reporting what others were saying about the Son of man, Jesus said, "But who do you say that I am?" It was upon Peter's confident affirmation, "You are the Christ," that Jesus said, "On this rock I will build my church" (Matt. 16:13-18). Each believer's personal witness is the means for sharing and imparting the good news.

Later, there was another instructive exchange between Jesus and Peter. Jesus asked repeatedly, "Do you love me?" If his love was more than casual and if, to the contrary, it was complete identification with the sacrificial ministry of Jesus, then Peter's task was inescapable. Firmly, simply, Jesus said, "Feed my sheep" (John 21:15-17). Each one's professed love for Christ must be lived out in service to those for whom Christ died

In the letter of 1 Peter, written to dispersed believers, we find one of the more exhalting, yet demanding, salutes to Christians: "You are a chosen race, a royal priesthood, a holy nation, God's own people, that you may declare the wonderful deeds of him who called you out of darkness into his marvelous light" (2:9). The chosen are a priesthood for service, not status—set apart for proclaiming God's action, not for claiming superiority.

No Lesser Roles

Ephesians 4 speaks of the inclusiveness of ministry in the New Testament community. There is "one body" just as there is "one Lord" and "one God," but Christians have various gifts to be used in "building up the body of Christ." Some have gifts for specialized leadership duties that include "equipment" of the whole church "for the work of ministry" (4-16). There is no question of who we are or what we do. There are no nominal or lesser roles. All share in ministry.

Over the centuries, this view of the ministry became distorted. There was a division of roles based upon the implied importance of the various functions to be performed. By the third century, bishops were firmly established over the clergy and the clergy had assumed authority over the laity. Since there were few books and schools, transmission of the gospel fell more and more to the professionals.

By the fifteenth and sixteenth centuries, it was evident that stratification of clergy and laity was a corruption. In this setting, Wycliffe saw the need for all believers to have access to the Bible and skill to read it. And Luther addressed himself to biblical grounds for "the priesthood of all believers." His thrust was not undoing the role of the priest (clergy), but rather was reestablishing the need for all Christians to see themselves as priests to one another. That role was not easily assumed by sixteenth-century lay people, however, for they lacked needed skills.

As the eighteenth century closed, there was ferment for further church reform in the young United States. Discontent with denominational exclusiveness was part of it. Some of the Protestant reformers, led by Barton Stone and Thomas and Alexander Campbell, joined forces in a movement that was to become the Christian Church. Functions of that group were performed by those at hand who were capable. Lay people preached, administered the sacraments and established the church in frontier communities. Congregations chose officers—elders, deacons and so on—and made corporate decisions. The mutual ministry of all believers contributed significantly to the Disciples' rapid growth.

Today, mission is fulfilled throughout the body of people, the laity and the clergy, in diverse yet mutual initiatives. We are using a biblical concept when we compare this to the specialized organs of the body acting as a single unit.

The ministry we share is based on and carried out in relationships. Our pattern is given to us by Jesus, who never lost sight of himself in relation to God and to other persons. As he began his ministry, Jesus read scripture aloud in the synagogue:

> "The Spirit of the Lord is upon me,
>   because he has chosen me to bring good news
>   to the poor.
> He has sent me to proclaim liberty to the captives,
>   and recovery of sight to the blind;

> to set free the oppressed,
>   and announce that the time has come
>   when the Lord will save his people."
> . . . "This passage of scripture has come true today, as you heard it being
> read" (Luke 4:18-21, TEV).

He proclaimed himself an emissary of God to the afflicted, the oppressed, and all who need to know that the time of salvation is now. As we share in his life and work, our concerns will be in a three-fold relationship—God, self, society.

God. We affirm the invitation for each of us to be a person of God.

God draws us into a personal relationship that is ever being enriched in meaning, vitality, and purpose. It might be compared to experiencing a symphony. At first the music is appreciated for its magnificent beauty, but with each hearing we are brought to new heights of understanding. And yet, there also is a majesty and mystery that can never be completely grasped or contained. Such is destined to be our relation to God—with each familiarizing encounter, also a greater mystery.

Liberating Obedience

In that relationship of mixed intimacy and awe, we are called to obedience to God's will. Discipline is fundamental to our sharing Christ's ministry. Jesus' apparent freedom in remaining steadfast to the end was first due to his responsiveness to God. Watching the flowing movements of a ballet artist, we are prone to applaud the dancer's seeming freedom and forget the years of controlled preparation which made it all possible. Our relationship to God will be liberating to the degree we are committed to his will.

Obedience is much more than following rules and submitting to authority. It is choosing the way of Christ and risking everything on God in sacrificial living. Marian Anderson, after years of mistreatment by society, was being honored by the city of Philadelphia for her outstanding contributions. Filled with emotion and unable to speak, she responded by singing a spiritual: "I open my mouth to the Lord, and I will never turn back. I will go, I shall go to see what the end will be." Being controlled by the Lord gives life its ultimate direction and freedom.

Self. As we who share in the ministry pursue a relationship with God, we also will seek self-fulfillment.

It is fortunate when we can see ourselves growing, for life is revealed in growth. Disciples believe in facilitating the process of development into Christian personhood. That's why so much emphasis is placed on nurture of the laity. One of the basic settings for maturing, which we recognize with much indebtedness, is the Christian family. Here the seeds are planted which ultimately will determine our lives. Here love, sacrifice, and forgiveness are first experienced. Without such experiences, we hardly can grow to love, care for, and forgive others.

As Jesus grew in wisdom, so must we. An astute observer in tune with Disciples thought observed, "The priesthood of all believers is noble, but ignorant priesthood is a travesty."[2] Education that contributes to the process of becoming is more than the acquisition of information. It also is gaining an understanding of one's attitudes, priorities, and habits, and the art of using them with discretion. So we always can be learning, whether in schools, church schools, conferences, fellowships, encounter groups, private reading, or penetrating devotional life.

As our faith is due in part to the witness of previous generations, so each of us is a link in sharing the faith story. Let us testify to our experience. To know and give evidence for what one believes is regenerative and rewarding. Note the vitality derived from lay persons writing Lenten devotional booklets, leading worship, and responding to inquiries in group sessions.

Laity is concerned not only with equipping self for ministry but also with organizing for service. This is done through the appointment of such church officers as elders and diaconate (we usually have said "deacons" and "deaconesses"), and structures like boards, task forces, and fellowship groups. These, along with the clergy, give leadership in establishing corporate goals in light of current needs and opportunities. Goal implementation is extended to all and response is according to dedication and ability. Beyond these ministries of the structured Christian community, the laity is engaged in ministry wherever responding in Christian service and witness.

Our Sphere of Influence

Society. Our target area is the world.

We remember that "God was in Christ reconciling the world to himself . . . and entrusting to us the message of reconciliation" (2 Cor. 5:19). Lay persons are eminently qualified to minister to the world by virtue of its being their sphere of influence. God's world is where we live, work, play, and dream.

When Jesus spoke of his ministry being to the poor, the captives, the blind and the oppressed, he was not looking at some remote, unusual condition of society. He was seeing life as it was all around him. In our day, society is marred by hunger, alienation, and injustice. There is a universality about the needs—a deep yearning in persons to realize their God-given dignity and worth in a community of love and acceptance. Our task is to respond individually and corporately by enabling others to become whole persons.

This is a self-giving ministry. It follows the pattern of Jesus. It avoids the pattern of paternalism or "super aid." We must be sensitive to our manner of sharing. Out of our present material abundance it is comparatively easy to care for hungry people at the moment, but the way we do it can leave the poor in a state of servitude rather than personhood. Also, it is apparent that poverty has become big business. It supports our affluence. The cry is for alleviating causes of inequities even though our opulence is threatened.

---

2. Ronald Bridges, "The Complete Layman" (commencement address delivered at Pacific School of Religion, Berkeley, Calif., June 2, 1950).

The Christian laity of the present Third World admonish us to see the extensive effects of our life-styles. There is urgent need to engage in reform of systems—economic, political, and judicial—in order that the people of the world might live more equitably and humanely. Recently, a Christian layman of the Dominican Republic made an appeal that American Christians endeavor to elect leaders "of the people, by the people and for the people" of the *world*.

Rather than angle for private advantage, we are expected to sacrifice for others. Teilhard de Chardin has stated:

> For in truth those will be saved who dare to set the center of their being *outside themselves*, who dare to love Another *more than themselves*, and in some sense become this Other: which is to say, who dare to pass through death to find life.[3]

Surely that will be our path if we follow Jesus in ministry.

Our thanksgiving for the ministry we share is expressed in the words of a hymn by Calvin W. Laufer:

> We thank Thee, Lord, Thy paths of service lead
>   To blazoned heights and down the slopes of need;
> They reach Thy throne, encompass land and sea,
>   And he who journeys in them walks with Thee.[4]

Grace Riddell Ford is a teacher of physical science in Spokane (Washington) Public Schools.

She is an elder in Spokane's Central Christian Church, where her husband, Gerald M. Ford, is pastor. In the summer of 1976, Mr. and Mrs. Ford made a study of poverty in the Caribbean.

Mrs. Ford served for five years on the board of directors of the International Convention of Christian Churches, and was a delegate to the 1966 General Assembly of the National Council of Churches.

A graduate in chemistry from Texas Woman's University, she formerly was an electro-chemist at the National Bureau of Standards, Washington, D. C. She is co-author of several patents, the most popular of which is the Electroless-Nickel Process.

3. Pierre Teilhard de Chardin, *Hymn of the Universe.* Harper & Row, 1961, p. 121.
4. Words copyright 1919, by Calvin W. Laufer, From "The Hymnal," 1933.

Some are set apart for servanthood

Eugene W. Brice

Few areas within the life of the Christian Church (Disciples of Christ) have seen as many significant developments within the past twenty years as has our concept of the Christian ministry. These developments derive from various forces both within and without the church.

In 1968, *A Provisional Design for the Christian Church (Disciples of Christ)* was adopted. The *Design* provided for a covenantal and structural relationship which bound the many Christian Churches into the one Christian Church. During the same decade, the cultural milieu in which the churches were operating also was experiencing change. Urbanization continued, with its corresponding decline of small towns and rural parishes. The rise of the women's liberation movement was seen. Personalistic and charismatic religious experience received new impetus, and with it, larger numbers of persons were interested in ministry.

Given these and many other important changes, it would have been remarkable, indeed, if our concept of Christian ministry had not been affected. Those forces still are being felt, of course, and they portend continuing adjustments within our ideas of ministry. Thus, a description of our concept of ministry is certain to be blurred, for it seeks to catch in a still photo what is a rapidly moving picture.

Nonetheless, let us make four assertions about our view of ministry and note very particularly the way in which denominational and cultural changes are challenging them.

I

We believe strongly in "the priesthood of all believers," but we are becoming more exact in our definition of who may be given standing as ordained ministers. In its section on "Ministry," the *Provisional Design* states our long-held belief: "By virtue of membership in the church, every Christian enters into the corporate ministry of God's people."[1]

While pioneer Disciples preachers would not have phrased this in such lofty terms, they believed it exactly. The democratic, almost populist, approach to ministry among Disciples in the nineteenth century was scandalous to some and attractive to many others. Distinctions between the privileges of ministers and lay persons in our early congregations were vigorously denied. Much of our growth in the late nineteenth century was due to lay persons who moved to new communities and, without benefit of ordained clergy, established congregations and led in mission and in worship.

This democratic approach to ministry continues in many respects today. Probably no other "mainline" Protestant church today gives more traditionally ministerial privileges to lay persons than does the Christian Church.

Yet it also is true that we now are setting more rigid requirements which a person must meet in order to receive standing as an ordained minister within the church. The *Provisional Design* provides that "The Christian Church, through the General Assembly, shall approve general policies and criteria for the order of the ministry . . ." and that "Within policies developed by the General Assembly, regions certify the standing of ministers. . . ."[2] This usually is done through a regional committee on the ministry. While each region interprets the "general policies" of the Christian Church on its own, most regions are moving toward strictly requiring, for example, a completed three-year graduate program in theology as prerequisite to ordination. Other requirements are personal recommendations with regard to character and faith, recommendations from a local congregation, and participation in an "ordination council" or conference. On the completion of these requirements, the candidate is recommended for ordination by the regional committee on the ministry. After ordination, the region certifies the minister's standing, which results in his or her being listed in the *Year Book and Directory* of the church as an active, recognized servant.

------

1. Section VI, "Ministry," *A Provisional Design for the Christian Church (Disciples of Christ)*. This document or its successor is available from the General Office of the Christian Church, P.O. Box 1986, Indianapolis, Ind. 46206.
2. *Ibid.*

Clearly, this represents a real shift in the locus of authority for ordination over the past two decades. One respected author wrote in 1956, "Our ministers become ministers by the action of local congregations of Christians. They are ordained by *local congregations* [italics his]. . . ."[3] Another wrote, "Once a congregation ordains a minister, his standing is never questioned by any other congregation. . . ."[4]

Our direction today is to recognize the mutual interest in ministry shared by the many congregations, the regions, and the general manifestation of the church—and thus the mutual responsibility for authenticating ministry. Ordination services still normally are held in congregations, but regions and congregations share responsibility for ordination. Whenever possible, representatives of the general and ecumenical church participate in the act of ordination. The region functions in behalf of the whole church in granting standing.

We note also that among the ministers of the Christian Church there is a movement toward a more careful definition of ministry. The Congress of Disciples Clergy, formed in the mid-seventies, is one such group that seeks to identify, organize, and serve the clergy.

So while our concept of the "priesthood of all believers" remains strong, we are becoming more careful in identifying those who are "set apart for servanthood."

II

We believe in a ministry carefully and highly trained in first-rate theological seminaries, but we are challenged by the problem that well over half of our congregations are so small that they find it difficult, if not impossible, to give adequate financial support to a full-time highly-trained minister.

Disciples are proud of the quality of the four theological seminaries directly related to the church—Brite Divinity School of Texas Christian University, Christian Theological Seminary, Lexington Theological Seminary, and the Graduate Seminary of Phillips University. The basic theological education (B.A. or B.S. followed by master of divinity) requires seven years for completion. In addition, our seminaries now are offering doctor of ministry degrees that require another year or two of study. In 1977, our four seminaries had 485 students studying for the M.Div. degree, and 193 for the D.Min. degree. Among them, our seminaries offer half a dozen other degrees including the master of religious education and the master of sacred theology, and their total enrollment in the fall of the 1976-77 school year was 859.[5]

In addition, we Disciples have three seminary foundation houses related to major interdenominational schools—Disciples Divinity House, University of Chicago; Disciples Divinity House, Vanderbilt University; and Disciples

---

3. Granville T. Walker, "About the Ministry," *What We Believe*, edited by James M. Flanagan. The Bethany Press, 1956, p. 102.

4. Howard E. Short, *Doctrine and Thought of the Disciples of Christ*. Christian Board of Publication, 1951, p. 74.

5. Statistics on 1976-77 enrollment are from *Disciples Seminarians Report* compiled by the Board of Higher Education of the Christian Church (Disciples of Christ).

Seminary Foundation, School of Theology at Claremont. They had 110 students in 1976-77.

Not all of the students in the Christian Church's seminaries are Disciples. But on the other hand, Disciples attend non-Disciples institutions. In 1976-77, a total of 734 Disciples were known to be enrolled in graduate schools continuing their ministerial preparation.

But even as our ministers reach for advanced degrees, and even as our seminaries grow in quality, we must ask: Who will serve the smaller congregations? In Oklahoma, New Mexico, and Texas, there are 684 Disciples congregations, of which 537 have fewer than 250 members, and 305 fewer than 100 members. Many persons have suggested that a congregation requires at least 250 members to give adequate support to a full-time minister and at the same time maintain program and mission.

We currently are developing answers to the problem of leadership for the smaller churches, and the next decade or two will grade our answers. In the future we doubtless will turn to pastoral "yoke" arrangements in which a minister serves two or more small congregations simultaneously. We may also need to make greater use of persons entering the ministry late in their lives from other vocations. Our seminaries, working with regional committees on ministry, will need to devise programs to give these persons needed training. Our structures will need to find ways to give them adequate ministerial standing. According to our present system, ordained ministers are given vote in the General Assembly[6] and in most regional assemblies, while licensed ministers working in full-time positions with congregations have no vote in the General Assembly—unless, of course, they are elected delegates. We will need to correct the implication of a second-class ministerial standing for some.

Through such steps as these, we can maintain our emphasis on a carefully trained, high-quality ministry and at the same time provide capable ministerial leadership for the significant number of smaller congregations in our midst.

III

We believe that women are fully eligible for and ought to be involved in ministry, but we are providing them with an insufficient number of positions in which to serve. Disciples long have accepted women for ordination. Yet our acceptance always has been more theoretical than real. Indeed, in a paper on ministry published as recently as 1964 in connection with a Commission on Brotherhood Restructure resource, a writer takes for granted that ministers will be men. He speaks of the ministry of "men with special gifts," of "our fathers' emphasis," of "these men" in ministry and of those churches unable to maintain a "fulltime man." Nowhere is there any hint of women in ministry.

Yet, in 1977, more than 25 percent of Disciples seminarians are women! This is especially startling in view of the fact that there are presently only about a dozen women serving as full-time preaching pastors of local Christian Churches. Our theory has been that women are fully eligible for any form of

---

6. *Ibid.* Section III, A, "The General Assembly," *Provisional Design.*

ministry, but our tradition has been to relegate them to the field of Christian education, and in an unjust but implied hierarchy, deny them the "top" spot of preacher.

There are factors which point toward a continuing improvement in this situation. One is the increasing number of Christian Churches elevating women to the eldership. Another is an innovative program, recently developed, which utilizes women ministers in interim ministries in local congregations. Still another is the increasing willingness of regional ministers to bring women to the attention of pulpit committees as they do their ministerial relocation work.

The next decade or two will show whether we can close the gap between our practice—exclusion of women from ministry—and our theory—full eligibility of women for ministry.

IV

We believe that the traditional responsibilities of parish ministry are important. Preaching, teaching, administration, and pastoral work are central as a minister gives primary attention to the upbuilding of the church. But we increasingly are seeing the minister as responsible for the development of human potential and for giving attention to ills of society that require creative treatment.

In repeated surveys taken among us, we continue to list preaching as the parish minister's most important responsibility. Pastoral, administrative, and educational tasks follow in close order. Yet we are seeing these tasks as more person-centered than we did in past years. Many of the terms now being used to describe the ministerial role point in this direction. Various authors recently have described today's minister as "shepherd," "pastoral director," "foreman," "enabler," "catalyst," "navigator," "coach" and "quarterback," among many others. All of these terms emphasize the minister's role in assisting church members toward personal growth and fulfillment.

The difficulty of the minister's task derives from the fact that the people he or she works with start from so many different places, and represent such a variety of interests and concerns. The minister today faces what has been called "the Moses misery," i.e., the responsibility for leading the whole people of God to the Promised Land of fulfillment through mission and service. Both the fast-moving enthusiasts and the slow-moving foot soldiers are included in this number. Through its ministry, the Christian Church seeks to serve this wide variety of people, recognizing that a variety of styles of ministry will be necessary.

Because of this, some ministers among us will be out on the edge of society, breaking new ground in mission for the church. Such ministries tend to arouse more controversy than others do, and they include frequent possibilities for both spectacular victories and embarrassing defeats.

Some ministers among us will be seen carefully guarding the rear echelons, emphasizing our heritage and surrendering ground very grudgingly.

Others—probably the majority—will be serving as bridges between the extremes. These ministers will be attempting to close the gap between where the people are and where the church ought to be. They will understand that it is the slow-moving, nurturing churches that produce the fast-moving, innovative prophets, and that these adventuresome prophets, in turn, breathe new life into the lagging churches. Through this kind of creative, but ofttimes trying, interaction, the church experiences a continuing renewal.

We do believe, then, that within the wider ministry of the people of God, there are those set apart for servanthood. Some of our traditions for ministry, well-founded in scripture and in practice, are valuable and creative, and they will continue. But some of the new realities of life today demand innovation and change. As we blend these two forces together, we wait to see where the Spirit, working through individual minister and corporate body alike, will lead us.

Eugene W. Brice has been pastor of First Christian Church in Tulsa, Oklahoma, since 1975.

Across the previous twenty years, he served four congregations in Texas—First Christian Church, Wichita Falls; Highlands Christian Church, Dallas; Handley Meadowbrook Christian Church, Fort Worth; and First Christian Church, Alpine—and spent 1960-63 at the Evangelical Seminary of Puerto Rico as professor of biblical languages and literature.

A former president of the Christian Church in the Southwest and a former member of the General Board of the Christian Church, Dr. Brice currently is secretary of the board of trustees of Brite Divinity School of Texas Christian University and a member of the board of the World Convention of Churches of Christ (Christian/Disciples). He serves on the boards of the Christian Church in Oklahoma and Oklahoma Christian Home at Edmond.

He earned B.A. and B.D. degrees from Texas Christian University and M.A. and Ph.D. degrees from Yale University.

A frequent Bible lecturer, he has contributed to *The Disciple, Pulpit Digest* and *Pulpit Preaching* magazines.

Christians serve their neighbors in love

Wallace R. Ford

Sooner or later, we find ourselves in the Plaza of Neighbor Love.[1] Granted, some of us are there reluctantly or at best uncertainly. But others of us have come enthusiastically, anticipating exploration of the avenues leading from the plaza. All of us are present because we heard a call, a voice, an invitation, to which we said a "Yes," no matter how tentative. The call came to us in different ways. For some of us, it came during a midnight prayer. For others the call was seeing a frail person whose face had been made lifeless by the ravages of malnutrition. For still others of us the invitation came when someone needing to unload a deep-felt hurt asked, "Do you have a minute?" Yet as we converse on the plaza, we find our common denominator: "Love your neighbor."

---

1. This phrase, "The Plaza of Neighbor Love," is the author's title for his figurative, almost poetic essay, which in keeping with the overall plan of this book is headed by a six-word affirmation of the basic belief it presents.—Editor.

So we mill around in preliminary conversations and take a minute to gaze at the statue in the plaza's center. We find ourselves staring at the inscription at its base: "Love one another, even as I have loved you." Suddenly a stranger introduces himself to us: he is the guide. He asks each of us why we are here. We tell him in our own words about the call. He nods and begins to explain the strange statue: "You will notice how the pioneer seems to point in all directions. The statue was carved late in the. . . ." His voice drones on. Only half-listening now, we thumb through the guidebook he gave us until our eyes pick out the words:

> [The social responsibility of the church is] that of the pioneer. . . . It is the sensitive and responsive part in every society and mankind as a whole. It is that group which hears the Word of God, which sees His judgements, which has the vision of the resurrection. In its relations with God it is the pioneer part of society that responds to God on behalf of the whole society. . . .
>
> It is the direct demonstration of love of God and neighbor. . . . It is the radical demonstration of faith. . . .[2]

Now, the guide, having completed his explanation, asks if we are ready to explore the avenues leading from the plaza in each direction of the compass. (My aim in this essay is to describe the pluriformity of neighbor love characteristically found among those of us who are members of the Christian Church and the point of essential unity as well. The encompassing imagery for this description is the *journey* we are making together.[3]) We all begin to choose which avenue we will explore first. And it becomes clear to us that though we will be going in different directions for awhile, we will return to this starting point, which is our unity.

Ethical Consensus

Directly to the north leads the Avenue of Ethical Consensus. As some of us journey this way, we discover that neighbor love at times is expressed through confrontations with issues that demand an ethical stance.

We Disciples are members of a voluntary association. Our history reaches back to the influence of John Locke, who described the ideal human community as a voluntary association of persons seeking their common prosperity. As this concept grew during the formation and westward expansion of the United States, the American church member became conscious of the importance of his or her personal faith journey. Individual Christians were admonished to develop their own convictions founded on experience and guided by scripture. Consequently, today, we Disciples do not easily acquiesce to proclamation by pulpit

2. H. Richard Niebuhr, "The Responsibility of the Church for Society," *The Gospel, the Church and the World*, ed. Kenneth S. Latourette. Harper & Brothers, 1946, pp. 130, 132.

3. This same imagery is used in the title of the definitive history, William E. Tucker and Lester G. McAllister, *Journey in Faith: A History of the Christian Church (Disciples of Christ)*. The Bethany Press, 1975.

or resolution. We expect to be a part of the consensus process, to be included in the shaping of decisions, to be convinced by pragmatic evidence. We firmly want to do the right and just thing, but simply being told what is right and just will not suffice.

Of course, the consensus process can be ignored. But the price is heavy: the will to belong diminishes. On the other hand, when the process heeds the individual's perspective, the strength of participation grows. Perhaps this partially explains how the "two or three" praying together over an issue of justice, of neighbor love, release new power. Certainly Jesus made clear that the decision to participate in his fellowship is a voluntary one made after a realistic counting of the cost (Luke 14:25-33). Once this insight dawns on us, we discover our companion who is walking with us.

In the congregation and in regional and general assemblies of the church, the development of ethical consensus is one means of expressing neighbor love. The time we spend in deliberation is not wasted, but moves us toward a position which all of us to some degree have had a part in developing. It has been observed that in ecumenical bodies—conferences and councils of churches and so on—the positions of all participating churches are strengthened in the process of arriving at consensus on a social issue. Representatives of the churches are enlightened in the exchange of opinion, and they gain a degree of assurance that whatever has been hammered out jointly is the closest they can come to what the Lord would have them say.

Justing Love

To the east lies the Avenue of Justing Love. Some of us choose to go up this avenue, almost like Diogenes, searching for ways to demonstrate concern for justice.

Once again we find Jesus making the journey with us. He began his ministry with a proclamation in his hometown:

> "The spirit of the Lord is upon me
>   because he has anointed me;
> he has sent me to announce good news to the poor,
> to proclaim release for prisoners
>   and recovery of sight for the blind;
> to let the broken victims go free,
> to proclaim the year of the Lord's favour.
>
> —Luke 4:18-19 (NEB)

John Yoder suggests that this "year of the Lord's favour" was Israel's Jubilee year.[4] If so, the search for justice is not a "social action tangent" to the gospel. Indeed, it is at the very center of submission and loyalty to the Kingdom. For the people of Israel, the Jubilee year (Lev. 25) provided a total renewal in which economic and social inequities built up over the previous fifty years were corrected. Yoder suggests further that since the Jubilee was so radical, it probably was not regularly observed and raised serious problems. Imagine cancelling all debts for one year in any community today (Deut. 15)! So when Jesus called for a return to Jubilee, he was met with hostility. Later, his pattern prayer for the forgiveness of *debts* attacked the paradigmatic social evil: inequality and domination. How revolutionary, how exacting our reenactment of the Lord's Prayer becomes when seen in this light!

The search for justice faces forthrightly the global issue of human rights. It unmasks the lies which states develop to excuse oppression in the name of national security. Through prayer and praxis (practical response or action) the loving neighbor urgently pursues the elimination of oppressive policies, wherever they might be, claiming loyalty to the Kingdom of God as a higher value than protection of national security.

Justing love is attuned to those crushed by systems in our communities. It looks critically at the deteriorating condition of our criminal justice systems; at benign agencies of social concern which, by their very systemic natures, allow people to "fall through the cracks"; at government subsistence payments which do not necessarily bring wholeness of life, and often prevent its realization; at the grand schemes of racism, sexism, and nationalism with their appealing scapegoats. Recognizing the institutional frame of witness, nurture, and service units of the church also, justing love watches for ways to make structures more responsive to human needs. The Christian neighbor gets involved in community and church agencies and endeavors, and participates in decision-making bodies such as boards and councils to work for social justice.

Already the imagination begins to grasp how the avenues are related, for in just this instance we discover the connecting streets between justing love and ethical consensus.

Suppose, for example, a Disciple identifies a particular form of injustice and brings it to the attention of his or her congregation. The issue is clarified and the praxis planned through the consensus process. This is the pioneer planning required to engage the setting in which the injustice is perpetuated. If appropriate or strategic, the larger church—regional, general (national/international) and ecumenical—can be involved in the redress of the injustice.

Among Disciples the joining of ethical consensus and justing love has produced concrete results. Congregations have sponsored housing projects to meet the need for decent places to live. Cooperating at many levels, we have started the homes and care centers of our National Benevolent Association. In a nationwide Mother-to-Mother Program, church women not only develop personal relationships with women who need friends but also become advocates. Examples are numerous.

---

4. John H. Yoder, *The Politics of Jesus.* Eerdmans, 1972, pp. 36f. Used by permission.

Witnessing Love

To the south lies the Avenue of Witnessing Love, that one-to-one relationship that is so rewarding.

Most of us in local congregations choose this avenue, but its popularity does not diminish its importance. Witnessing love may be sharing over a cup of coffee another's joys, hurts, loneliness, or despair. It may be taking time each week to transport an elderly person for cancer treatment at a clinic. It may be the ministry of listening when someone calls and asks, "Can I speak about something troubling me?" It may be reading scripture to someone searching for meaning and purpose in life. It may be witnessing to one's own journey through dark valleys and to discovery of the One who walks with us. It may be visiting in a home with someone who recently visited our church. It may be the long-term support of a refugee family or an unemployed father looking for work. The list could go on and on.

Sometimes bone weary, sometimes dancing with joy, we travel clogged side streets responding to calls, making ourselves available, expecting to care. God has planted that care in our hearts, and thereby is transforming us. Even when bitten or rejected, the Christian neighbor does not give up his or her compassion.

There are congregations that sponsor telephone reassurance programs, develop skills banks to match members' abilities and interests with human needs, and recruit volunteers for community programs. Congregations establish day-care facilities for children, youth, and senior adults; counseling centers for the distressed; vocational counseling services; and support groups for the divorced and the recently widowed. Individual members provide foster care for children and help for ex-convicts. This list, too, expands miraculously.

To the west lies the Avenue of the Ochlos, *the lost and least.* Jesus' preference for them sometimes strains our desire to be neighbor. We would choose the Sermon on the Mount (Matt. 5) over the Sermon on the Plain (Luke 6). Yet it is there—his compassion for the *ochlos,* who are the ones who have no power, no redress, no shepherd.

Down this avenue we look at faces peering from the hovels of life. Those who by accident of birth are the dispossessed call out to us, "Son of David, have mercy on me." Once in a while, one of us steps out to comfort the dying, clothe the naked, or visit the sick or the imprisoned.

Perhaps what is required first is for us to let the *ochlos* evangelize *us,* get through all the protective devices we create. Here is humanity's stark condition—deprived of rights, comfort, food, housing, let alone self-esteem and beauty. The voice calls out: "Look closely. Let them speak to you. This is not what I intended for my children."

When we have looked and when we have ministered "to one of the least of these" (Matt. 25:40), we discover the unique double brotherhood of Jesus. For he stands joining our hands with those of the least and the lost, the no-people who are his people. On this involvement with the least through Christ, William J. Nottingham comments:

. . . people who accept Christ as their personal Lord and Savior are also accepting the poor of this world as their brothers and sisters. They enter into communion with God and find that he has called them to be responsible in the struggle for a better life for all. . . . The Holy Spirit leads some to love their neighbor, suffer indignation at needless oppression, forgive their enemies, but resist evil, and search for new models of society.[5]

Global Network

The side streets now are seen for what they are, channels in a global network of compassion. Out of the ethical consensus, the concern for justice and the wanting to be in touch with the neighbor, emerges our linkage with the *ochlos*.

Through these streets the church receives information about human needs and sends resources of compassion. In providing emergency assistance to victims of natural disasters, education to illiterate hill people, medicine for sick children and community resources for peasants and refugees, we share neighbor love with brothers and sisters around the world. Money we give and prayers we share touch the lives of so many, sustain so many, encourage so many. This network, for example, enables my hand to touch the poor and the powerless served by Friendship Mission in Asuncion, Paraguay. More than a million other Disciples join me in helping to create a more humane community there, even though none of us participate directly in the mission's day-to-day life.

We Disciples find ourselves asking, "What makes this journey so difficult? Why is neighbor love something we resist?" Here we must acknowledge what we are up against. Hovering in every alley of each avenue is the Temptor.

Just as Jesus was, we are tempted to pick up bread and eat: "Lay up for yourself sufficient goods, then you can care about others." The Temptor offers us vistas of influence: "It's essential now to build your cities of security and importance, so amass your diplomas, accomplishments and positions before turning to your neighbor." Then he comes with a subtle temptation: "Leap away from the demanding consequences of love's claim." A longing lies within us to delay and avoid: "Lord, that young man burned out on drugs is too demanding, too frightening. Let me walk by on the other side." He may graciously allow that to happen, but not before making sure we see the one lying there on the side of the road.

From our confrontations we learn the servant style. Servanthood does not come easily or naturally. Give us the choice between the style of a towering pine and that of a mustard bush, and the heroics will be hard to set aside. Let some dissident voice attack our "program" and watch our strident defense. But our distinctive name, "Disciples of Christ," connotes our willingness to explore the way of servanthood.

Somewhere along the way, we come across his amazing grace, his rain that doesn't stop at the fence of the righteous. And we learn that mercy is at the center of life itself and that we are called to be ambassadors of that charismatic mercy.

---

5. William J. Nottingham, "The Biblical Basis of Evangelism as Mission," *Biblical Basis for Evangelism.* Christian Board of Publication, 1976, p. 69.

Community

Returning, we make yet another discovery: In being neighbor, we participate in creating that kind of community which is the foretaste of the Kingdom. Slowly we come to understand how the "belonging" each of us wants involves communication, and how communication creates community as we risk giving ourselves to others. Community is the persistent persuasion of God's love in and through us. It requires sacrifice, attendance to our common environment, acknowledgement that all have a right to share the resources of life. The alternative is the attempt to save one's life, which means losing it. In community, love is participation, not possession.

Now we return to the plaza. How surprised we are to discover it transformed! The statue is gone, replaced by a great feast. Seated around the tables are those we met on the journey: the board member who argued with us over nuclear energy, the city council member to whom we addressed our concern about the jail, the Latin American whose well we helped dig, the woman we talked with over the phone, the lost and hungry man we barely could look at, the youth we assisted in job-hunting.

"Come, blessed of my Father," the host (we recognize him now as the guide) at the far end of the table calls, "you are properly dressed in the garb of a servant."

"But," we stammer, "when did we see you . . . ?"

"Enter," the host reassures us. "Enter into the joy of my double brotherhood. For people will come from east and west, from north and south to sit at table for my feast."

Wallace R. Ford has been pastor of First Christian Church, Boulder, Colorado, since 1967. He previously served the LaPorte (Texas) Community Church for three years.

He has headed the Boulder Council of Churches, the Boulder Communication Center and the community Social Services Advisory Committee.

His current involvements include the local Criminal Justice Advisory Committee, Emergency Housing of Boulder and Community Hospital Chaplain Associates.

Mr. Ford also serves on the Criminal Justice Commission, Colorado Council of Churches; the Outreach Commission, Boulder Council of Churches; and the department of evangelism, Central Rocky Mountain Region of the Christian Church.

A third-generation Disciples minister, he earned B.A. and B.D. degrees from Texas Christian University and is working toward a D.Min. degree at Iliff Seminary.

The church must make unity real

Ann Updegraff

In the past few years, it has been interesting to observe reactions to the use of first-century forms of worship. Practices such as foot-washing and the kiss of peace have been viewed by many as "new" and "radical" developments which are disruptive and not in the spirit of Christian worship. A closer look, of course, shows that such activities were a part of the church's beginnings and that their use demonstrates a reaching back into tradition for meaningful and creative ways to live out the experience and vision of Christian community.

In a similar way, discussion of church union in recent years has been viewed with confusion and mistrust. It has seemed to many members of the Christian Church that all this talk of a uniting church comes from those who do not understand what the church is all about. But in fact, as we will see in this chapter, the unity of Christ's church has been for Disciples a place of beginning as well as a destination: it has been a gift from the past as well as a mandate for the future. It is not only where we ought to be going and where we have been—it is where we began!

A bit of history is in order here. Perhaps the most appropriate place for us to look first is to the Scriptures, to see "where the Scriptures speak."[1] The vision of oneness is lifted up in many places in the New Testament, but nowhere so clearly as in that gentle and tender portion of the Gospel of John containing Jesus' prayer for his disciples and for all of his people. In his petitions to the Creator are these words:

> "I pray not only for them, but also for those who believe in me because of their message. I pray that they may all be one. Father! May they be in us, just as you are in me and I am in you. May they be one, so that the world will believe that you sent me" (John 17:20-21 TEV).

This prayer for unity at such a crucial time in Jesus' life—the time when he is preparing his disciples to carry on without him and preparing himself for what is to come—does not leave us much room to argue or hedge. The mandate is clear! It comes with the force of a command! And those who participated in the formation of the Christian Church understood that very well.

For Barton W. Stone, Thomas and Alexander Campbell and other early leaders, unity was the "polar star"[2] of the Christian Church as it emerged in the early decades of the nineteenth century. The very reason that this extraordinary pioneer movement of Christians began to take shape lay in the pain of separation that the founders experienced. They were *for* Christian union and *against* what they identified as causes and perpetuators of divisions in the body of Christ.

"The Last Will and Testament of the Springfield Presbytery," the work of Stone and his partners in ministry around Cane Ridge, Kentucky, in 1804, presented those concerns clearly. A statement against sectarianism, it expressed a desire for the Springfield Presbytery (formed only ten months earlier by six ministers who sought mutual support from one another without the theological strictures of regular Presbyterian organizations) to "die, be dissolved, and sink into union with the Body of Christ at large; for there is but one Body, and one Spirit, even as we are called in one hope of our calling."[3]

Five years after the signing of the "Last Will and Testament," Thomas Campbell, writing for the newly-formed Christian Association of Washington in western Pennsylvania, set down his hopes for a whole church united on the basis of the Bible. His *Declaration and Address* was a booklet which, like the "Last Will and Testament," developed out of the earnest questioning and sharing of a community of people as well as from the struggles and faith of an individual.

---

1. This phrase asserting the authority of the Bible is from a statement attributed to Thomas Campbell, a Disciples founder, which has been quoted frequently and applied variously.

2. This is a Barton W. Stone phrase that became part of the standard rhetoric of Disciples speakers on Christian unity.

3. "The Last Will and Testament of the Springfield Presbytery" (1804), complete text in William E. Tucker and Lester G. McAllister, *Journey in Faith: A History of the Christian Church (Disciples of Christ)*. The Bethany Press, 1975, pp. 78.

Proposition 1 asserted:

> That the church of Christ upon earth is essentially, intentionally, and constitutionally one; consisting of all those in every place that profess their faith in Christ and give obedience to him in all things according to the scriptures, and that manifest the same by their tempers and conduct, and of none else, as none else can be truly and properly called Christians.[4]

Later that year, when Alexander Campbell left Scotland and joined his father, it became clear that the two of them had reached similar conclusions about the church, though they had been separated by time and distance.

Quest for Wholeness

Stone in Kentucky and the Campbells in Pennsylvania developed followings, and these groups gained identities. The intent definitely was *not* to further fragment the church. Their public speaking, their journalism (publications were influential), and their evangelizing all promoted the goal of unity on New Testament grounds. When movements of the Campbells and Stone joined forces in the 1830s, the growing Christian Church's quest for wholeness was a primary focus.

The cause of unity has been lifted up time and time again in the Disciples history, but never more forcefully than in 1910, when Peter Ainslie, then president of the General Convention, called Disciples to recommit themselves to the search for unity. Ecumenical involvement of the Christian Church with other communions was advanced through his influence. The Council on Christian Union (now the Council on Christian Unity) was formed, and with a renewed sense of history as well as destiny, Disciples continued to uphold the objective of union.

In recent years, however, "uphold" evidently has meant talk to some and action to others. The church has, for the entire period of its existence, struggled with how much of its heritage to take seriously and how much to ignore, to keep at arm's length, to discuss but not deal with in terms of life and work. The world's critique of the church—that we often talk a good line while doing nothing—is particularly painful in the area of unity. And yet, though we may not see all of the action from either pulpit or pew, things *are* happening!

Since its inception, the Council on Christian Unity, now a general unit of the Christian Church, has promoted and articulated the vision and process of union. The journal *Mid-Stream,* published by the council, is read and respected globally by people seeking to share in and understand the action of God in the ecumenical movement. The council has for some years sent senior fraternal workers to the staff of the World Council of Churches, and has supported the WCC in other ways by supplying leadership to its various units and divisions. It is through the Council on Christian Unity that we Disciples are represented in conversations and dialogues with other churches. This merely is a sampling of

4. *Declaration and Address of the Christian Association of Washington County, Washington, Pa.* (1908), Prop. 1 Excerpts are quoted and sources of the text are cited in Tucker and McAllister, *Op. cit.* chap. 5.

the activities of the unit created to ensure that the Christian Church would persist in its quest for the unity of the church.

Since 1963, Disciples in the United States have been full participants in the Consultation on Church Union (COCU), which in 1977 involved ten bodies seeking a united church "truly catholic, truly evangelical and truly reformed." In the mid-seventies, the COCU strategy has been to encourage those of us in the participating churches to "live our way toward union." Touching all areas of church life, this process of achieving unity by experiencing it has included shared mission approaches, interim eucharistic fellowships (gatherings at the Lord's Table by Christians who are not ordinarily together there), generating communities (genuine grass-roots models of union that are alive and kicking *now*), consideration of mutual recognition of members, joint efforts and conversations among denominational entities at regional and national levels, and much more. Simultaneously COCU has been working carefully toward theological consensus through the drafting, discussion, and revision of a document entitled *In Quest of a Church of Christ Uniting*. The thrust of COCU is not merely toward efficient ways of working together, but toward actually being *one*.

U. S. Disciples continue to be serious about considering union with the United Church of Christ. Conversations were started before COCU was on the scene and were suspended for several years to allow both churches to focus on the more inclusive consultation. These discussions are characterized by a delicate tension between the vision of unity shared by the two churches and reality, between eagerness to fulfill the Lord's prayer for oneness and caution. Beginning in 1969, Canadian Disciples were involved in separate negotiations toward a three-church union in their country; and when talks involving the Anglican Church ended in 1976, meetings between the remaining participants, the Christian Church and the United Church of Canada, began.

International bilateral conversations between Disciples and the Roman Catholic Church were beginning in 1977. National bilateral talks between the two churches had started in the U.S. in the sixties. Such discussions are for the development of *communion* between the churches, not union—at least not soon.

For many years churches overseas that were begun as missions of North American Disciples have been losing their denominational identities in united churches. This is an exciting kind of fulfillment of our dream of Christian unity. In Zaire, for example, the united *Eglise du Christ au Zaire*, composed of fifty-three former denominations and missions, is headed by I. B. Bokeleale, who came from the Disciples community. Practically everywhere abroad, Disciples work through united churches or ecumenical bodies and agencies.

From our local communities to the world scene, we Disciples continue to be involved in councils of churches and other ecumenical organizations. We belong to both the National Council of Churches in the U.S.A. and the Canadian Council of Churches as well as the World Council. Much as we make practical use of local interchurch agencies for such programs as jail chaplaincies and broadcasting, we treat the National and World Councils of Churches as integral parts of our work in fields ranging from disaster relief to social justice.

Blurred Vision

Something we struggle with is how to give shape and substance to the insights, resolves, and platitudes about Christian unity that fill our history and our rhetoric.

Consider what happens in our communities. Though people in congregations of various denominations work together eagerly on certain projects, often through local councils of churches, somehow the discomfort increases when real talk of union takes place. While few of us Disciples would disagree outright with the view that we all *should* be one, someday, we seem to hang back from the "brass tacks" of church union.

Why? It seems to me there are several reasons.

One reason, I think, is that we have trouble imagining what unity would look like. We may have some sense of our heritage and a vague idea of what we should be working toward, but that doesn't really translate into our day-to-day experience. We are going to have to do something about that! If we can say with the Campbells, Stone, and their associates that Christ's divided body is a denial of the wholeness that he brings, then we have to be prepared to take some risks, to venture out and to explore the newness with one another.

That must have been the feeling of the early Christians themselves as the church began to grow and take shape a couple of thousand years ago. Traditions and practices evolved without a road map, without a pre-planned structure, without even a curriculum! Nobody said, "I won't participate until I know what it will look like!" Those first Christians were pioneers—in the same way that Stone and the Campbells were pioneers, and in the same way that we are called to be pioneers.

Too, among us, there seems to be a growing desire to protect what is "ours"—a feeling that what we have built needs to be cared for more than it needs to change and grow. The early church had nothing more than a nation and its heritage to move beyond; besides our understandings of the New Testament and our traditions, we have buildings, budgets, institutions, and structures. It is ironic that the sin of denominationalism, which prompts us to be conservative, is the very thing we Disciples came into existence to overcome.

But, when we are honest with ourselves, the truth shows through; behind the anxieties and the self-protectiveness, the vision is intact. We Disciples believe in unity. We support it. We are struggling to make it part of our lives as well as our history. We are aware that to be the church in the world is to be unable to rest until the church is *one*—Christ's body restored to its wholeness and Jesus' prayer for unity made a reality in spirit and in structure.

Healing in a Broken World

How does a divided church presume to bring a message of wholeness and healing to a broken world? How can a fragmented church speak convincingly about the evils of racism, sexism, economic exploitation, and nationalism? What does the church say to other sections of society when its own structures perpetuate separation between the able and the disabled, women and men, oppressors and oppressed, "our" culture and "theirs"?

These were among the tough questions dealt with in the 1975 Nairobi Assembly of the World Council of Churches.[5] Theme of that assembly was "Jesus Christ Frees and Unites," and just about every way of thinking about it was represented by the approximately 3,000 participants from almost 300 church bodies in some 100 nations. The diversity of the gathering made even more striking a report on unity proposing that congregations "share the same baptism and eucharist [Lord's Supper] and recognize each other's members and ministries."[6] Asking why the churches should not move rapidly, the report twitted, "And if the answer is 'because we are not yet united,' the question comes again: 'Then why do we not unite?' "[7] That's putting it the way a Disciple in the tradition of Stone and Ainslie would.

To live in hope of unity means to look to the past for a mandate and to the Spirit for direction. We Disciples are striving, in our better moments, to do just that.

Ann Updegraff has been associate minister of First Christian Church, Sacramento, California, since 1975. While writing this chapter in 1977, she was acting executive minister there.

Reared in Fort Lauderdale, Florida, she was ordained there in 1973. She was associate minister of First Christian Church, New Castle, Indiana, in 1974-75.

Ms. Updegraff served on the General Board of the Christian Church, 1973-76, and is on the training and care commission of the Christian Church in Northern California-Nevada. She has been regional youth resource person in Northern California-Nevada.

A member of the board of directors of the Disciples' Council on Christian Unity, she has been a delegate to three plenary meetings of the Consultation on Church Union and is chairperson of the consultation's Women's Task Force.

She earned degrees from Transylvania College and Vanderbilt Divinity School, where she was student body president.

<hr>

5. Reports on the 1975 Nairobi Assembly of the World Council of Churches are presented in *Mid-Stream*, Vol. XV, No. 2 (April 1976), Council on Christian Unity. The council is a source of other information on various ecumenical relationships of Disciples.

6. *Ibid.*, p. 218.

7. *Ibid.*, p. 219.

We look to the future hopefully

Carnella J. Barnes

"Let your hope keep you joyful," Paul wrote in his letter to the Christians at Rome (12:12 TEV).

It seems to me that we Disciples have a healthy measure of joy based on hope. We are not silly Pollyannas unable to see danger, grimness, and suffering in the real world around us. But neither are we long-faced, hand-wringing fatalists. We are joyful because we have hope.

We Disciples are long on optimism. We always have been.

The nineteenth-century movement that became the Christian Church spread rapidly on bold optimism. Prominent founders—particularly Alexander Campbell, Barton W. Stone, and Walter Scott—in contrast to Calvinism, believed that human beings were *not* hopelessly mired in sin, but could take steps prescribed in the New Testament to lay claim to God's promises of forgiveness, and new and eternal life. The founders also had confidence in the ability of the whole membership of the church, not merely the ordained ministers, to wield authority. Above all, they believed that a church divided into denominations along lines of opinion and tradition could be reunited by a return to the simple ways of the New Testament church. The Disciples' early optimism about humanity's participation in its own reclamation, democratic government, and restoration of church unity fit the mood of a young nation advancing westward to new beginnings and unbounded vistas.

Throughout our history, we Disciples have been willing to start ambitious, even fearsome ventures without knowing for sure what the outcome would be. The creation of the Christian Woman's Board of Missions in 1874 is an example. That organization of women initiated work now carried on through the Christian Church's Divisions of Homeland and Overseas Ministries, and has been succeeded by our Christian Women's Fellowship. But its origin was in an "untimely time," Lorraine Lollis, teller of the story of Disciples women, points out.[1] The general missionary organization of the church, led by men, was faltering, women still were second-class persons in the church as well as in society (suffrage for women was almost half a century away), and few had much money. In those unpromising circumstances, Caroline Neville Pearre and her sisters in the faith launched out—hopefully.

Similarly, optimistic Disciples started the revolving loan fund that became the Board of Church Extension (1883), a ministerial relief effort that produced the Pension Fund (1885), the National Benevolent Association and its homes for children and the aged (association in 1887, first home in 1889), and the forerunner of the Council on Christian Unity (1910).[2] With some doubts and forebodings as well as confidence, Disciples participated in the formation of organizations that have merged into the National and World Councils of Churches, and numerous local and regional ecumenical organizations. This merely is a smattering of examples from a century and a half chock full of beginnings powered largely on hope.

Confidence in Humanity

We Disciples have great confidence in humanity, particularly persons committed to "the best way of all"—love (1 Cor. 12:31b; 13 NEB). We affirm with Paul that "There is nothing love cannot face; there is no limit to its faith, its hope, and its endurance" (13:7 NEB).

Sharing the popular nineteenth-century view that religion and knowledge are essential to good government and human happiness, Disciples participated vigorously in the proliferation of schools and colleges in the United States. In fact, so many were founded that the grass-roots movement could not support them all. The nineteen surviving liberal arts colleges and universities related to the Disciples' Board of Higher Education are effective in training leaders. Reflecting characteristic Disciples thought, a recent annual report of the Board of Higher Education says, "The church is involved in ministries in higher

---

1. Lorraine Lollis, *The Shape of Adam's Rib*. The Bethany Press, 1970, esp. chaps. 1-3.
2. William E. Tucker and Lester G. McAllister, *Journey in Faith: A History of the Christian Church (Disciples of Christ)*. The Bethany Press, 1975, esp. chap. 11.

education by design; it has much in common with the enterprise of higher education, historically and intentionally, in meeting today's societal needs and tomorrow's future."[3]

Another sign of the faith we Disciples have in human beings is our changing approach to work overseas. There was a time when missionaries from North America and Europe always were the initiators, planters, and managers of churches and institutions in other countries. Missionaries made most, if not all, of the major decisions. Now the Christian Church in the United States and Canada is assuming the role of "partner" or "enabler" or "servant" in relation to self-governing churches in former "mission lands." "We hope . . . ," Robert A. Thomas, president of the Division of Overseas Ministries, wrote in explaining this stance, "that both the financial and personal resources we have to share will empower persons and institutions to serve their fellows, free their spirits, develop their capacities to be more productive and self-sufficient, and help their nations achieve a greater degree of justice and humaneness."[4]

At home, the Christian Church has adopted a church structure that could not even have been considered without confidence in people. We operate under a design that provides for three "manifestations" of the church—congregation, region and general (national/international) organization, each with full authority to function in its own sphere of responsibility.[5] All that holds us together is a covenant—not a legal document, but a commitment to care for one another. We Disciples firmly believe that church people can function as a whole body of Christ *voluntarily*.

In recent decades, racial minorities and women have been encouraged to participate more fully in the life of the Christian Church, particularly in leadership and decision-making. This is increasing the cultural and spiritual wealth of the church as well as its capacity to serve. To assure that the church adequately serves and involves minority constituencies, a Committee on Black and Hispanic Concerns regularly reviews the work of the whole church and makes suggestions.[6] In a series of resolutions, the 1973 General Assembly called on congregations to recognize a single diaconate (not separate groups of deacons and deaconesses) and urged increased service opportunities for women ministers.[7] With rare exceptions, care is taken to include minority persons and women in boards and committees throughout the Christian Church.

---

3. Annual Report, Board of Higher Education, *Year Book and Directory of the Christian Church (Disciples of Christ)*, 1975 ed. General Office of the Christian Church (Disciples of Christ), 1975, p. 103.

4. Robert A. Thomas, *Where in the World Are We Going?* Christian Board of Publication, 1973, p. 53.

5. *A Provisional Design for the Christian Church (Disciples of Christ)*. This document or its successor is available from the General Office of the Christian Church, P. O. Box 1986, Indianapolis, Ind. 46206.

6. "Minutes," General Board of the Christian Church (Disciples of Christ), June 12-15, 1976, Chicago, Ill.,GB-76-0363, p. 11.

7. "Minutes of the Third Biennial General Assembly of the Christian Church (Disciples of Christ), Cincinnati, Ohio, October 26-31, 1973," *Year Book and Directory of the Christian Church (Disciples of Christ)*, 1974 ed., ress. 37, 39 and 42, pp. 155, 157 and 161-62.

Optimism About Programs

We Disciples are optimistic about what can be accomplished through programs devised and run by church people. Examples:

- *Reconciliation,* a domestic program in which we combat racism and poverty in hopes of improving human relations and the quality of life for all children of God.
- *Disciples Peace Fellowship,* an organization of individuals committed to getting nations to solve problems and work out differences without arms stockpiles and war.
- *National Interfaith Coalition on Aging,* an ecumenical agency which, among other things, inspires services *with* (not merely services *to*) the aging, employing their experience, interests and talents.
- *Church World Service,* an agency of the National Council of Churches in the U.S.A. which aids victims of drought, natural disasters, wars, disease, and poverty globally.

Still, we do not pretend to be self-sufficient. As Paul wrote concerning the source of power for his own ministry:

> There is nothing in us that allows us to claim that we are capable of doing this work. The capacity we have comes from God; it is he who made us capable of serving the new covenant. . . . (2 Cor. 3:5-6 TEV.)

As confident as we Disciples are that human beings following Christ can make tremendous differences, our basic trust is not in the best of our programs but in God, the Creator and Ruler of the universe.

We believe in the ultimate victory of right over wrong. God demonstrated this certainty in the triumph of Christ over death. Jesus' life was goodness—love—in the flesh. He lived out servanthood. He washed his disciples' feet. He cared for society's outcasts. He treated each person as worthy of recognition and development. He taught that purity and righteousness involve more than surface cleanliness. He forgave. He healed. He turned people around. Then he was crucified. But that was not the end. He still lives!

Against problems that look overwhelming at the moment, we Disciples stack the certitude that the creation is endowed with still-undiscovered possibilities. We have not reached the limits of human potential. And there is no end to the resources of God, who is in charge. We look to the future with hope.

Carnella J. Barnes is an ordained minister whose career has spanned public school teaching, religious education, community service, and work with the aging.

During the 1974-78 quadrennium, she is president of International Christian Women's Fellowship—the first black to hold that office. With her husband, Anderson, she has served as elder in United Christian Church, Los Angeles.

A participant in the 1975 Nairobi Assembly of the World Council of Churches, Mrs. Barnes serves on the governing board of the National Council of Churches and the national board of Church Women United. She also is a trustee of the Disciples' National Benevolent Association.

She joined the United Christian Missionary Society staff in 1938 as a national field secretary and left that post seven years later to become executive secretary of the Avalon Community Center in Los Angeles. For three years beginning in 1958, she was minister of education at McCarty Memorial Christian Church, Los Angeles.

From early 1962 until retirement, Mrs. Barnes was an employee of the Los Angeles County Department of Senior Citizens Affairs in supervisory and executive positions.